**EXILE
AND
RETURN**

EXILE
AND
RETURN

Charles F. Pfeiffer

BAKER BOOK HOUSE
Grand Rapids 6, Michigan
1962

PHOTOLITHOPRINTED BY CUSHING - MALLOY, INC.
ANN ARBOR, MICHIGAN, UNITED STATES OF AMERICA
1962

CONTENTS

PREFACE

Between 600 and 400 B.C. — the era covered in the present study — the world received much of its present religious and philosophical inheritance. During the time of Judah's Exile, the Persian religious leader Zoroaster was developing his dualistic concepts which were to become the state religion of Persia until the Mohammedan conquest. At about the same time, Confucius, the Chinese sage, was born in what is now Shantung Province; and Buddha Gautama, born into an environment of luxury in India, determined to lead the ascetic life and, as a result, developed the principles of Buddhism.

Both the Neo-Babylonian and the Persian empires, successively, reached the zenith of their power during these centuries. Before they were over, Greece had proved her ability to resist encroachments from the East at Marathon (490 B.C.); Persian power was checked; and the tide of empire began to move westward. The noblest achievements of Athenian culture found expression during the Age of Pericles (461-429 B.C.) . Socrates (469-399 B.C.) and Plato (427-347 B.C.) were developing their philosophies before the close of our period and, before the end of the next century Hellenism was to dominate the East.

Important changes were also taking place among the Israelites. Judah, the Southern Kingdom, had maintained a precarious existence for almost a century and a half after the fall of her northern neighbor, Israel, to Assyria in 722 B.C. When the armies of Nebuchadnezzar finally breached the walls of Jerusalem (587 B.C.), Judah, as a political entity, was absorbed into the Neo-Babylonian Empire, and most of her people were taken into Exile.

The Exile was the water-shed between ancient Israel as a political unit and the religion known as Judaism. The Jews of the post-exilic period had their spiritual roots in the institutions and prophetic utterances of their earlier history. Political Israel, however, had been anchored to a geographical area and a civil ruler in a way which differed markedly from post-exilic Judaism. Although Jews of the dispersion (i.e., those away from Palestine) loved Zion and sent their gifts to the paternal homeland, the institution of the synagogue, which developed after the destruction of the First Temple (587 B.C.), made corporate Jewish life possible in any land. The Jew might look forward to the coming of a messianic ruler of the Davidic line, but he adapted to the rule of Babylonians, Persians, and their successors.

The present study is concerned with the religious, cultural, and political life of Exilic and Post-exilic Judaism. Our history extends from Nebuchadnezzar, whose armies brought the First Jewish Commonwealth to an end, to Nehemiah, whose leadership in the rebuilding of the walls of the restored city injected a new spirit of enterprise among the Jews of his day. The culture of ancient Babylonia is a focus of attention for the understanding of the Exilic Age. The Persian Period is given fuller treatment in the author's *Between the Testaments* (Grand Rapids: Baker Book House, 1959).

It has been the purpose of the writer to lend historical perspective to the Biblical text. To do this he has had to draw heavily on the work of others. The books mentioned in the Bibliography have been constant companions, and the writer acknowledges his indebtedness to their authors. He hopes that this study will enable the reader to gain an appreciation of the backgrounds of the Exile and the Post-exilic Age.

Charles F. Pfeiffer

Beverly Farms, Mass.

EXILE
AND
RETURN

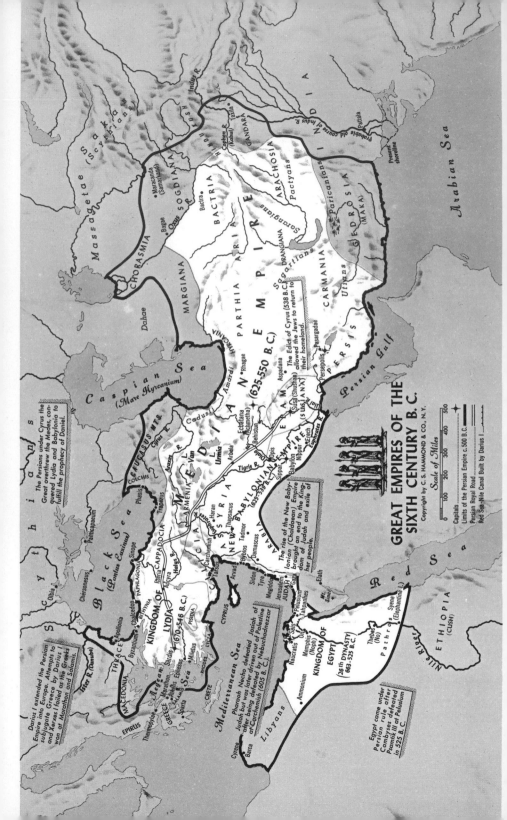

GREAT EMPIRES OF THE
SIXTH CENTURY B.C.

Copyright by C. S. HAMMOND & CO., N.Y.

Scale of Miles

0   100 200 300 400 500

Capitals
Limits of the Persian Empire c.500 B.C.
Persian Royal Road
Red Sea-Nile Canal Built by Darius I

Arabian Sea

Massagetae (Scythians)

The Persians under Cyrus the
Great overthrew the Medes, conquered Lydia and Babylonia to
fulfill the prophecy of Daniel.

CHORASMIA

SOGDIANA
Maracanda (Samarkand)
Bagae
Oxus R.
Bactra
BACTRIA
ARIA
Kophen R. (Kabul)
GANDARA
Taxila
Indus R.
Pattala
Present old course of Indus R.
Present shoreline

ARACHOSIA
Pactyans
Drangiana
Sarangians
Sagartians
GEDROSIA (MAKA)
Paricanians
CARMANIA
Utians
PERSIS
Persepolis
Pasargadae

The Edict of Cyrus (538 B.C.)
allowed the Jews to return to
their homeland.

MARGIANA

Dahae

Caspian Sea
(Mare Hyrcanium)

Rhagae
Amardi
PARTHIA
EMPIRE
HYRCANIA
625-550 B.C.

Aspadana
Persian Gulf

Cadusi
MEDIA
Ecbatana (Hamadan)
Behistun
Susa (Shushan)
ANZAN
Opis
Sippar
Babylon
Nippur
Erech
Euphrates R.
Tigris R.

ARMENIA
Van
Urmia
Arbela
ASSYRIA
Nineveh
NEW BABYLONIAN EMPIRE
605-538 B.C.

CAUCASUS MTS.
Cyrus R.
COLCHIS
Phasis
Trebizond
Araxes R.

Black Sea
(Pontus Euxinus)

Panticapaeum
Chersonesus
Olbia

Scythians

Darius I extended the Persian
Empire into Europe, to subjugate
the Scythians. Attempts to
subdue Greece by Darius I
and Xerxes I failed as the Greeks
won at Marathon and Salamis.

THRACE
Ister R. (Danube)
MACEDONIA
Byzantium
Chalcedon
Apollonia
EPIRUS
Thermopylae
GREECE
Athens
Marathon
Salamis
Sparta
Aegean Sea
CRETE
RHODES
SAMOS
Ephesus
Miletus
Sardis
LYDIA
KINGDOM OF LYDIA (670-546 B.C.)
PHRYGIA
PAPHLAGONIA
Sinope
CAPPADOCIA
Pteria
Mazaca
Halys R.
PISIDIA
LYCIA
CYPRUS

Sinai
CILICIA
Tarsus
Carchemish
Haran
Thapsacus
Tadmor
Byblos
Damascus
Sidon
Tyre
Megiddo
Samaria
Jerusalem
JUDAH
Gaza
Pelusium
Mt. Sinai

The rise of the New Baby-
lonian (Chaldaean) Empire
brought an end to the Kingdom of Judah and exile of
her people.

Pharoah Necho defeated Josiah
of Judah but was later driven out
of Palestine after being defeated by
Nebuchadnezzar at Carchemish (605 B.C.)

ARABIA

Mediterranean Sea

Cyrene
Barca
Libyans
Ammonium
Naucratis
Memphis (Noph)
KINGDOM OF EGYPT
663-525 B.C.
26th DYNASTY

Tahpanhes
Sais
Daphnae
Syene (Elephantine I.)
Thebes (No)
Pathros

Red Sea

ETHIOPIA (CUSH)
Nile River

Egypt came under
Persian rule after
Cambyses defeated
Psamtik III of Pelusium
in 525 B.C.

1

THE CAMPAIGNS OF NEBUCHADNEZZAR

The center of power in the Tigris-Euphrates Valley period-ically shifted. The Amorite lawgiver, Hammurabi, ruled from ancient Babylon during the eighteenth century B.C. With the decline of the Old Babylonian Empire, the political center moved northward and the Assyrians came to control not only Babylon but most of Western Asia. Sargon II (721-705 B.C.) es-tablished his capital at Nineveh, and his successors marched east-ward to the Mediterranean in quest of tribute and booty.

The Assyrians were humbled by the Chaldeans, a Semitic peo-ple who had been in Babylon since about 1000 B.C. Nabopolas-sar (626-605 B.C.) threw off the Assyrian yoke and founded an independent Chaldean, or Neo-Babylonian Empire. Not only were the Assyrians unsuccessful in putting down his revolt, but they lost their own capital, Nineveh, when Nabopolassar joined forces with Cyaxeres the Mede in 612 B.C. The Assyrians re-treated westward to the ancient city of Haran, but it too fell to the Babylonians and their allies (610 B.C.). The following year Pharaoh Necho of Egypt (609-593 B.C.) marched northward to Carchemish on the Euphrates to assist the Assyrian king, Ashur-uballit, in an effort to retake Haran from the Babylonians. Josiah of Judah sought to prevent Necho from marching his troops through the Valley of Jezreel, but Josiah was killed in a battle fought at the fortress of Megiddo. The effort to regain Haran for the Assyrians failed, and Assyrian power was never felt again. Babylon took its place as a world power. Egypt, however, saw an opportunity to gain control of Syria and Palestine. Necho de-posed Jehoahaz, the son of Josiah, after a short reign of but three months. Eliakim, a brother of Jehoahaz was appointed king of Ju-dah by Necho, who renamed him Jehoiakim.

Nabopolassar died in 605 B.C. shortly after his son Nebuchadnezzar[1] had defeated the Egyptians at Carchemish and,
again, at Hamath. Nebuchadnezzar returned to Babylon to
claim his throne. It may be that he sent his armies to secure
the allegiance of the peoples of Syria and Palestine at that time.
This would explain the reference in Daniel 1 to exiles taken
to Babylon during Jehoiakim's reign.

We possess records of the campaigns of Nabopolassar and
Nebuchadnezzar for the twenty-three year period between 616
B.C. and 594 B.C. in the Chaldean Chronicle.[2] It contains a
report of the Battle of Carchemish (605 B.C.) :

> In the twenty-first year the king of Akkad stayed in his own land. Nebu-
> chadrezzar his eldest son, the crown prince, mustered the Babylonian
> army and took command of his troops; he marched to Carchemish which
> is on the bank of the Euphrates, and crossed the river to go against the
> Egyptian army which lay at Carchemish . . . . He accomplished their
> defeat and to non-existence beat them. As for the rest of the Egyptian
> army which had escaped from the defeat so quickly that no weapon had
> reached them, in the district of Hamath the Babylonian troops overtook
> and defeated them so that not a single man escaped to his own country.
> At that time Nebuchadnezzar conquered the whole area of the Hatti-
> country. For twenty-one years Nabopolassar had been king of Babylon.
> On the 8th of the month of Abu he died; in the month Ululu, Nebu-
> chadrezzar returned to Babylon and on the first day of the month Ululu
> he sat on the royal throne in Babylon.[3]

The Chronicle speaks of a series of campaigns in "the Hatti-
country" or Syria. In his first year as ruler of Babylon we read,
"All the kings of the Hatti-land came before him and he received their heavy tribute."[4]

Another cuneiform inscription boasts of the accomplishments
of the king:

> In exalted trust in him (i.e., Marduk, god of Babylon), distant coun-
> tries, remote mountains from the upper sea (Mediterranean) to the lower
> sea (Persian Gulf), steep paths, blockaded roads, where the step is im-
> peded, where was no footing, difficult roads, desert path, I traversed, and
> the disobedient I destroyed; I captured the enemies; established justice

---

1. The Babylonian form of the name is Nabu-kudurru-usur, which approxi-
   mates the Biblical Nebuchadrezzar, the form of the name frequently used
   in Jeremiah and Ezekiel. The Old Testament historical books, and Daniel, use the form Nebuchadnezzar.
2. D. J. Wiseman, *Chronicles of Chaldaean Kings:* (626-566 B.C.) *in the
   British Museum.* See also David Noel Freedman, "The Babylonian Chronicle," *The Biblical Archaeologist,* XIX, 3, pp. 50-60. Dr. Freedman's
   article appears as Chapter 10, *The Biblical Archaeologist Reader* (edited
   by G. Ernest Wright and David Noel Freedman).
3. Wiseman, *op cit.,* pp. 67-69.
4. Wiseman, *op. cit.,* p. 25.

in the lands; the people I exalted; the bad and evil I separated from the people.[5]

Nebuchadnezzar subdued the Lebanon mountain region and established his sovereignty there. The trail which he took in ascending the Wadi Brissa can still be followed. As we go up the gorge from the Riblah plain we reach a place where the rock is smooth. On one side we see a relief of Nebuchadnezzar standing before a cedar, and on the other he is depicted warding off a lion. His accomplishments are described in a nearby inscription:

> Trusting in the power of my lords, Nebo and Marduk, I organized my army for an expedition to the Lebanon. I made that country happy by eradicating its enemy everywhere. All its scattered inhabitants I led back to their settlements. What no former king had done, I achieved: I cut through steep mountains, I split rocks, I opened passages, and thus I constructed a straight road for the (transport of the) cedars. I made the Arahtu float down and carry to Marduk, my king, mighty cedars high and strong, of precious beauty and of excellent dark quality, the abundant yield of the Lebanon, as (if they be) reed stalks (carried by) the river. Within Babylon (I stored) mulberry wood. I made the inhabitants of the Lebanon live in safety together and let nobody disturb them . . .[6]

Nebuchadnezzar continued southward to the Dog River which enters the Mediterranean north of Byblos. Near the mouth of the river three Egyptian and four Assyrian inscriptions already commemorated the prowess of Nebuchadnezzar's predecessors. On its north bank Nebuchadnezzar inscribed a copy of the Wadi-Brissa Inscription.

The smaller states of Syria and Palestine were easy prey for Nebuchadnezzar. His real foe and potential rival was Egypt. During Nebuchadnezzar's fourth year, the Chronicle tells us, he marched against Egypt. The battle seems to have been indecisive, for each side inflicted heavy casualties upon the other. Nebuchadnezzar was sufficiently weakened that he found it necessary to return to Babylon.[7] Since he had been the aggressor, it could be considered a defeat for Babylon.

During the period of Nebuchadnezzar's advance in Syria and Palestine, Jehoiakim of Judah paid tribute to the Babylonians (II Kings 24:1). When Nebuchadnezzar was forced to return home after his unsuccessful attempt to subdue Necho of Egypt,

---

5. Translated from G. A. Rawlinson, *Cuneiform Inscriptions of Western Asia*, I 33, col. 11, line 12 ff. in G. A. Barton, *Archaeology and the Bible*, p. 478.
6. From the so-called Wadi-Brissa Inscription. Translation adapted from A. Leo Oppenheim, "Babylonian and Assyrian Historical Texts," James Pritchard, ed. *Ancient Near Eastern Texts*, p. 307.
7. Wiseman, *op. cit.*, p. 71.

Jehoiakim rebelled, trusting Egypt to come to his aid if necessary. The year following the Egyptian fiasco, Nebuchadnezzar "stayed in his own land and gathered together his chariots and horses in great numbers."[8] His absence from western Asia doubtless strengthened the hands of the pro-Egyptian groups.

Judah's respite was short, however. In December, 598 B.C. the Babylonian army was on the march again. The same month, Jehoiakim died. It is likely that he was assassinated (cf. Jer. 22:18-19; 36:30) by Judaeans who hoped to placate Nebuchadnezzar. The Chronicle reads:

> In the seventh year, the month of Kislimu, the king of Akkad mustered his troops, marched to the Hatti-land, and encamped against (i.e., besieged) the city of Judah (i.e., Jerusalem), and on the second day of the month of Addaru he seized the city and captured the king. He appointed there a king of his own choice, received its heavy tribute and sent them to Babylon.[9]

Jehoiachin, the eighteen-year-old son of Jehoiakim, who had succeeded to the throne at the death of his father, reigned but three months before Jerusalem surrendered to Nebuchadnezzar and he was taken to Babylon (II Kings 24:12). The "king of his own choice" whom Nebuchadnezzar placed on the throne of Judah was Mattaniah (II Kings 24:17), an uncle of Jehoiachin. Nebuchadnezzar gave him the name, Zedekiah. The exiles looked upon Jehoiachin as their legitimate king, however. Dates were reckoned "from the exile of King Jehoiachin" (Ezek. 1:2). Babylonian administrative documents list provisions assigned to individuals who were prisoners of war or, for other reasons, dependent upon the king. Among those who receive provisions is *Ya'u-kinu* king of *Yahudu*.[10]

The Chaldean Chronicle closes with the eleventh year of Nebuchadnezzar (594-593 B.C.). From other sources, however, we are able to piece together the trouble-filled years preceding the fall of Jerusalem. When Pharaoh Necho died (593 B.C.) the Palestinian states of Edom, Moab, Ammon, Tyre, and Sidon met at Jerusalem (Jer. 27:3), hopeful that the new Egyptian ruler, Psammetichus II, would aid them in a fresh challenge to the power of Babylon. Psammetichus pursued a policy of non-interference, however, and the plot against Babylon proved an embarrassment to Zedekiah, who was evidently its leader. The Judaean king journeyed to Babylon (Jer. 51:59) and swore allegiance to Nebuchadnezzar.

8. *Ibid.*
9. Wiseman, *op. cit.*, p. 73.
10. See p. 21-22.

Zedekiah is not an attractive character. Although at times he seems to have been "more sinned against than sinning," Zedekiah was guilty of vacillation. Jeremiah urged him to remain loyal to Nebuchadnezzar, but the pro-Egyptian party in court called for rebellion. Loyal Judaeans thought of Nebuchadnezzar as an oppressor, and many false prophets joined in the plea for Judah to assert its independence. At the death of Psammetichus II (588 B.C.), his successor, Apries (Biblical Hophra) decided upon a more energetic participation in Asiatic affairs. He gained control over the Phoenician cities and encouraged a league of Palestinian states to resist Babylon. Zedekiah succumbed to the pro-Egyptian party in his court and became a participant.

Nebuchadnezzar reacted swiftly. By January, 588 B.C. (II Kings 25:1; Jer. 52:4), Jerusalem was under siege (Jer. 21:3-7). From his headquarters at Riblah, on the Orontes River, Nebuchadnezzar was able to take the Judaean strongholds, one by one, until only Lachish, Azekah, and Jerusalem were left (Jer. 34:6-7). A glimpse of life during these difficult times is given in the Lachish Letters, a collection of pieces of broken pottery inscribed with ink, discovered by the late J. L. Starkey at Tell ed-Duweir, southwest of Jerusalem. Tell ed-Duweir is now identified with Biblical Lachish.

The letters reflect conditions outside the capital in a way comparable to Jeremiah's description of things in Jerusalem itself. A tragic note appears in the fourth letter which concludes:

And let (my lord) know that we are watching for the signals of Lachish, according to all the indications which my lord hath given, for we cannot see Azekah. (See illustration on page 16.)

The writer of the letter was probably with the Judaean fighters in the field.[11] The signal of which he speaks was probably a fire signal, as the Mishna suggests. The writer gave the sad news that the signal from Azekah had failed. Evidently the city had fallen to Nebuchadnezzar's army.

There was one glimmer of hope left for Judah. Egypt might yet come to her rescue and challenge Nebuchadnezzar. As a matter of fact Egypt did march northward: "The army of Pharaoh had come out of Egypt; and when the Chaldeans who were besieging Jerusalem heard news of them, they withdrew from Jerusalem" (Jer. 37:5).

When Pharaoh Apries' forces advanced into Judah, the pro-

---

11. See Chapter 5.

Lachish Letter IV. The Lachish Letters indicate the military situation in Judaea in the months prior to the fall of Jerusalem to the Babylonians. In Letter IV a field commander reported that the signals from Azekah were no longer visible. Azekah had evidently capitulated. Soon afterward both Lachish and Jerusalem were occupied by Nebuchadnezzar's armies.

Egyptian nobles felt that their policies were vindicated. Only Jeremiah injected a sour note, prophesying defeat for Judah (Jer. 37:6-10; 34:21). Jeremiah, however, was right. Nebuchadnezzar turned back the Egyptian force and resumed the siege of Jerusalem.

During the summer of 587 B.C. the end came. The army of Nebuchadnezzar breached the walls of the city which was facing starvation in any event. The Babylonian king's patience was exhausted. He determined to raze and burn the city and appointed Nebuzaradan, the captain of the guard, to oversee the destruction of Jerusalem. The Temple treasure was pillaged and the city walls were reduced to rubble. The Temple, palace, and other buildings were completely destroyed. Zedekiah attempted to escape toward Ammon (II Kings 25:3-4; Jer. 52:7-8), but he was taken near Jericho and brought to Nebuchadnezzar's headquarters at Riblah. There Zedekiah witnessed the execution of his sons before he was blinded and taken in chains to Babylon (II Kings 25:6-7) where he died.

Nebuchadnezzar determined that Judah should never again challenge his authority. He sent a commander, Nebuzaradan, to Jerusalem with orders to destroy the city. Jerusalem was burned and its walls leveled. Military, civil, and religious leaders were executed at Riblah (II Kings 25:18-21) and less dangerous elements in the population were exiled to Babylon.

The poor peasants of Judah were permitted to remain in the land which, as a matter of fact, was completely desolate (II Kings 25:12). To keep some semblance of order among them, Nebuchadnezzar appointed a Judaean noble named Gedaliah to govern the remnants of Judah from Mizpah, north of the ruins of Jerusalem. A seal discovered at Lachish identifies Gedaliah as chief minister in Zedekiah's cabinet. His father, Ahikam, had once saved Jeremiah's life (Jer. 26:24), a fact which may show his sympathy with Jeremiah's desire to co-operate with Nebuchadnezzar.

Gedaliah's reign was short-lived, however. He was regarded as a collaborationist because he attempted to "do business" with Nebuchadnezzar. A member of the Judaean royal house named Ishmael gained the backing of the king of Ammon and plotted to kill Gedaliah. Although warned of danger, Gedaliah refused to believe the reports he heard about Ishmael.

Ishmael, however, went through with his plans. Joined by his fellow conspirators he attacked Gedaliah, killed him along with members of a Babylonian garrison stationed at Mizpah, and a number of the Jews who were nearby. Although pursued by Gedaliah's men, Ishmael made good his escape to Ammon. The surviving Judaeans, fearing reprisals from Nebuchadnezzar because of this treachery, determined to flee to Egypt. Jeremiah urged them not to do so, but they could not be dissuaded, and Jeremiah, himself, was forced to accompany them there.

Mention is made of a further deportation of Judaeans in 582 B.C. (Jer. 52:30). This may have been brought on by the disorders which followed the murder of Gedaliah. Neither the Scriptures nor Babylonian records give any hint concerning the length of Gedaliah's governorship, although it appears to have been of short duration. With the death of Gedaliah and the dispersion of the surviving Judaeans, corporate Israelite life in Palestine came to an end. The bulk of the territory once belonging to kings of the Davidic dynasty was probably incorporated into the territory of Samaria, one of the provinces of the Babylonian Empire.

Nebuchadnezzar had begun the siege of Tyre the year before the fall of Jerusalem. Ittobaal III, however, was able to withstand Nebuchadnezzar and his generals for thirteen years. As the great commercial city of the eastern Mediterranean, Tyre was supplied by sea and was not crippled by Nebuchadnezzar's land blockade. Tyre could boast "I am a god. I sit in the seat of the gods in the sea's midst" (Ezek. 28:2). Tyre occupied both a site on the Phoenician mainland and an island one-half mile from the shore. In time of siege, the Tyrians moved to their island and, protected by a large and efficient navy, they felt themselves impregnable.

In 574 B.C., Tyre was forced to come to terms with Nebuchadnezzar. Ittobaal abdicated his throne in favor of Baal II (574-564 B.C.) and a nominal Babylonian suzerainty was recognized. Tyrian business documents after that time were dated in the year of Nebuchadnezzar.

Nebuchadnezzar also subdued the Ammonites and destroyed their capital city, Rabbah. Jeremiah had prophetically described its desolation:

> Therefore, behold, the days are coming, says the Lord,
> When I will cause the battle cry to be heard
> against Rabbah of the Ammonites;
> it shall become a desolate mound,
> and its villages shall be burned with fire;
> then Israel shall dispossess those who dispossessed him,
> says the Lord (Jer. 49:2).

The Ammonite king was taken as a captive to Babylon. A few years after the capitulation of Tyre, Nebuchadnezzar undertook a campaign against Egypt (568 B.C.) and defeated Amasis but made no attempt to penetrate into Egypt.

2

JUDAH'S LAST KINGS

The death of good King Josiah brought to a close an era in Israelite history. His reign had been marked by revival. During the latter days of his rule the Assyrian Empire was destroyed and Nahum could glory in the destruction of the enemy of God's people — and of all western Asia. Neither the spiritual revival nor the defeat of Assyria had permanent effects on the future of Judah, however. Idolatrous kings were to nullify Josiah's spiritual impact, and the Chaldean or Neo-Babylonian Empire would become heir to Assyria as the threat to the East.

1. Jehoahaz

The people of Judah did not realize the changes which were in store for them following Josiah's death. His younger son, Jehoahaz (or Shallum), was anointed by "the people of the land" (II Kings 23:30) who expected him to continue a policy of friendship with Babylon and political independence for Judah. Jehoahaz, however, reigned but three months (609 B.C.). Pharaoh Necho, whose armies had been responsible for the death of Josiah at Megiddo, deposed Jehoahaz and imprisoned him in the Egyptian camp at Riblah (II Kings 23:33). Leaving an army of occupation in Syria and Palestine, Necho took Jehoahaz to Egypt where he subsequently died. Eliakim, his older brother, renamed Jehoiakim, was appointed by Necho to rule Judah. Jehoiakim evidently was pro-Egyptian in his sympathies, and was ready to become a vassal to Necho. This may be the reason that he had been passed over in favor of his younger brother at the time of Josiah's death.

2. Jehoiakim

Jehoiakim's loyalty to Egypt proved costly to his subjects in

Judah. The heavy tribute he was forced to pay certainly became
a drain on the national economy:

> And Jehoiakim gave the silver and the gold to Pharoah, but he taxed
> the land to give the money according to the command of Pharoah. He
> exacted the silver and the gold of the people of the land, from every one
> according to his assessment to give it to Pharaoh Necho (II Kings 23:35).

Judah, as a vassal state, doubtless faced serious economic
problems. The equivalent of over two million dollars had to be
paid to Egypt. Tribute is never easy to pay, and the irresponsi-
bility of Jehoiakim did not help matters. Early in his reign he
built a new palace, using forced labor (Jer. 22:13-14 R.S.V.).
Expensive cedar paneling and costly paint added to its mag-
nificence. Jeremiah looked upon this as symptomatic of a heart
that was not right with God. He warned:

> O inhabitant of Lebanon,
> nested among the cedars,
> how you will groan when pangs come upon you,
> pain as of a woman in travail! (Jer. 22:23).

The reformation associated with Josiah had never been popular, and subsequent events seemed to discredit it. The death
of Josiah would be regarded by those who had no sympathy with
his reformation as a divine judgment upon one who had effected
religious change. Man constantly asks, "If he was right, why
was he taken?" Then, too, times were hard. Some looked back
to days before the revival and felt that they were better off then.
They said to Jeremiah:

> As for the word which you have spoken to us in the name of the Lord,
> we will not listen to you. But we will do everything that we have vowed,
> burn incense to the queen of heaven and pour out libations to her, as
> we did, both we and our fathers, our kings and our princes, in the cities
> of Judah and in the streets of Jerusalem; for then we had plenty of food
> and prospered and saw no evil (Jer. 44:16-17).

Along with the lapse into idolatry there arose a false confidence in the inviolability of Jerusalem and its Temple. Had
not God entered into covenant with David saying, "Your house
and your kingdom shall be made sure for ever before me; your
throne shall be established for ever" (II Sam. 7:16)? False prophets were saying to the people of Jerusalem, "He will do nothing;
no evil will come upon us, nor shall we see sword or famine"
(Jer. 5:12).

In 605 B.C. Nebuchadnezzar defeated the Egyptian army at
Carchemish, on the Euphrates River. He followed them southward to Hamath on the Orontes where they suffered a second
defeat. The following year Nebuchadnezzar was back in Syria
and, by the end of 604 B.C. his armies were in control of the
Philistine Plain. Jehoiakim, seeing Nebuchadnezzar so close,

broke his ties with Egypt and offered to become a vassal to Babylon (II Kings 24:1). He was a vassal through expediency, not loyalty. As soon as Nebuchadnezzar suffered a reversal, urged on by the pro-Egyptian party at court, Jehoiakim rebelled. The act was a foolish one, for Nebuchadnezzar promptly dispatched against Jehoiakim "bands of the Chaldeans, and bands of the Syrians, and bands of the Moabites, and bands of the children of Ammon" (II Kings 24:2). Then, in December, 598 B.C. the Babylonian armies were ready to march against Judah. While Jerusalem was under siege, Jehoiakim died. Jeremiah had prophesied, "With the burial of an ass he shall be buried, dragged and cast forth beyond the gates of Jerusalem" (Jer. 22:19). Probably Jehoiakim was murdered by his own courtiers who hoped thereby to gain some favor from Nebuchadnezzar.

3. Jehoiachin

Jehoiachin, the eighteen-year-old son of Jehoiakim was ill prepared to lead his people when he took the reins of government. Within three months after Jehoiachin became king, Jerusalem surrendered to the Babylonians (II Kings 24:12). The young king was taken to Babylon along with his queen mother, palace officials, artisans, and other leaders in the community. Ezekiel, later to become known as the great prophet of the Exile, was taken captive at this time.

Young Jehoiachin seems to have been looked upon as the legitimate king of Judah even though he was succeeded in Jerusalem by his uncle, Zedekiah. Jehoiachin remained in Babylon as a political prisoner for thirty-seven years. We are told that Evil-Merodach, Nebuchadnezzar's successor, "graciously freed Jehoiachin king of Judah from prison and he spoke kindly to him, and gave him a seat above the seats of the kings that were with him in Babylon" (II Kings 25:27-28).

The fact that Jehoiachin was given a food allowance by the Babylonian king (II Kings 25:29-30) is mentioned in Babylonian cuneiform records. Three hundred dated tablets found years ago in the ruins of a vaulted building near the famed Ishtar Gate were published in 1939 by Ernst F. Weidner, then of Berlin. They list payments of rations from the government to captives and skilled workmen who were in Babylon from 595 to 570 B.C. Included are people from Egypt, Iran, Media, Asia Minor, Phoenicia, the Philistine cities, Syria, and Judah. Among

the latter we read of *Ya'u-kinu* of the land of *Yahudu*, i.e.,
Jehoiachin of Judah, together with his five sons.[1]

Discoveries in Palestine also illustrate the position of Jehoiachin. Three stamped jar handles have been discovered (two at
Debir and one at Beth-shemesh) bearing the Hebrew inscription,
"Belonging to Eliakim, steward of Yaukin." These discoveries
lead us to believe that a man named Eliakim was custodian of
the property of Jehoiachin while he was in Babylon. The exiled
king's possessions seem to have been kept intact, and there were
doubtless many who hoped that he would soon return and
replace Zedekiah.

4. Zedekiah

When Jehoiachin was taken to Babylon, he was succeeded in
Jerusalem by his uncle Mattaniah whom Nebuchadnezzar renamed Zedekiah. Zedekiah was expected to be a puppet of
Nebuchadnezzar. He ruled a land whose cities had been severely
damaged, whose population had been in part deported, and
whose economy was certainly crippled.

An abler man might have used his energies in rebuilding his
nation, leaving strictly political matters for later consideration.
Zedekiah's position was, to be sure, difficult. He seems to have
been well-intentioned, but he could not resist the counsel of his
nobles and the clamor of the populace. Egypt was constantly
offering aid to encourage Judah to rebel against Babylon.

The nobles who surrounded Zedekiah were inexperienced.
Those wise in the way of government had gone to Babylon with
Jehoiachin. The very fact that Jehoiachin was in Babylon added
indirectly to the troubles of Zedekiah. If, as the false prophets
declared, the exiles would soon return, then Zedekiah must be
prepared to meet Jehoiachin's challenge to his throne.

The exiles did not return. Instead Zedekiah's problems arose
from his own princes who, in the words of Ezekiel, were "like
wolves tearing the prey, shedding blood, destroying lives to get
dishonest gain" (Ezek. 22:27). The nationalistic, pro-Egyptian,
anti-Babylonian party soon gained royal support. By the fourth
year of Zedekiah's reign we find him in consultation with ambassadors from Tyre, Sidon, Edom, Ammon and Moab — all of
whom were bitterly anti-Babylonian. At about this time Zede-

---

1. W. J. Martin, "The Jehoiachin Tablets," in D. Winston Thomas, *Documents from Old Testament Times*, p. 86.

kiah journeyed to Babylon (Jer. 51:59). Perhaps Nebuchadnezzar heard rumors of defection and wanted to discuss matters with Zedekiah. Evidently Zedekiah was able to satisfy Nebuchadnezzar of his loyalty.

Open rebellion was not long in coming, however, Zedekiah made an alliance with Egypt, the hereditary enemy of Babylon. A new Pharaoh, Apries (Biblical Hophra) had come to the throne of Egypt in 588 B.C. He determined to invade Palestine and establish Egyptian suzerainty there. Ezekiel describes these events: "But he [Zedekiah] rebelled against him [Nebuchadnezzar] by sending ambassadors to Egypt that they might give him horses and a large army" (Ezek. 17:15). Nebuchadnezzar took note of Zedekiah's treachery, and sent an army into Judah. Soon the whole countryside except the cities of Azekah, Lachish, and Jerusalem, was in Babylonian control (Jer. 34:7).

Egypt made a feeble attempt to come to the aid of her ally. The Babylonians who, by this time had laid siege to Jerusalem itself, were forced to turn their forces toward the Egyptian border. For a moment it appeared that Jeremiah, who had urged loyalty to Babylon, was wrong and deliverance would come from Egypt. The hope was ill-founded. The Egyptian force was driven back by the might of Nebuchadnezzar, and the siege of Jerusalem was resumed.

From this moment on, the situation of Jerusalem was hopeless. Zedekiah realized that Jeremiah was right, but the king feared it was too late to surrender (Jer. 38:14-23). Famine and pestilence devastated the city before it was finally taken by the enemy. In July, 587 B.C., Nebuchadnezzar's armies breached the walls of Jerusalem. Zedekiah fled toward the Jordan, doubtless hopeful of a place of sanctuary in Ammon. He was captured near Jericho and taken to Nebuchadnezzar who was encamped at Riblah in central Syria. There, after witnessing the execution of his sons, Zedekiah was blinded and taken to Babylon in chains.

3

EGYPT AND THE EXILE

When Necho II became Pharaoh of Egypt (609 B.C.) he dreamed of restoring his land to the glories which it had enjoyed during its great Empire Period. Psammetichus I, his father, had taken the throne of Egypt with the blessings of Ashurbanipal of Assyria. Ashurbanipal, however, was plagued with troubles in Babylon, Arabia, and Asia Minor, and could not prevent Psammetichus from ridding himself of his Assyrian counselors and adopting an independent course of action. Psammetichus built an army of mercenaries, including Greeks who began to enter Egypt in large numbers during his reign. Greeks came to Egypt as merchants and in the western Delta they established communities which became manufacturing centers. Memphis and other large cities had Greek quarters. Strabo states that the first settlements of Greek traders from Miletus took place during the reign of Psammetichus. On the eastern edge of the Delta the Greeks were encouraged to establish the trading post which they named Daphne (Biblical Tahpanhes, Jer. 44:1). It served as a frontier fortress defending Egypt from attack from the east.

Other foreign merchants were permitted to settle in Egypt under Psammetichus. The sea-going Phoenicians sent their galleys to the mouths of the Nile Delta. Aramaeans from Syria were welcomed as permanent settlers, as were Carians, Lydians, and other peoples of Asia Minor. The Jewish mercenaries who are known to have been in Elephantine, at the first cataract of the Nile, during the fifth century B.C., may have come to Egypt during the reign of Psammetichus I, although some scholars date their arrival in Egypt at the time of Psammetichus II (593-588 B.C.). Egypt became a prosperous land, and Psammetichus dreamed of empire. By 640 B.C. Psammetichus I was ready to dispute Assyria's claim to Syria and Palestine. He invaded the Philistine territory and took Ashkelon with little difficulty. Ashdod was secured after a twenty-nine year siege. Although faced with opposition from the Scythian invaders, Psammetichus was able to restore Egypt to a position of strength which it had not enjoyed since the days of Ramesses III (1175-1144 B.C.).

With the fall of Nineveh (612 B.C.), Egyptian interests demanded a change in policy. No longer was Assyria the villain in the plot to keep Egypt weak. Babylon was the new rival, and the Egyptians determined to check Babylonian power at all costs. One of the first acts of Necho, as Pharaoh, was to march his army toward Carchemish in a vain effort to help the Assyrian, Ashur-uballit, to retake Haran from the Babylonians. It was during this march that Necho passed the Israelite stronghold at Megiddo and killed Josiah of Judah who was seeking to prevent the Egyptians from joining forces with Assyria against Babylon.

On his way north from Megiddo, Necho, aided by his Greek mercenaries, took the Syrian city of Kadesh-on-the-Orontes. He showed his appreciation for the help of the mercenaries by dedicating the garments worn during the victorious battle in the Temple of Apollo at Branchidae in Miletus.

Although unable to prevent the Babylonians from taking over the eastern portions of the Assyrian Empire, Necho was able to control for himself much of Syria and Palestine. Josiah's son, Jehoahaz was sent to Egypt in chains after a three month rule over Judah. Eliakim, another of Josiah's sons, was installed as Necho's puppet, and renamed Jehoiakim. Judah was forced to pay one hundred talents of silver, and one of gold, as tribute to Necho.

Necho's purposes were soon to be thwarted, however, by the young Chaldean prince, Nebuchadnezzar, who was heir to the throne of Babylon. When Necho attempted to defend his Syrian dominions at Carchemish (605 B.C.), Nebuchadnezzar's armies gained a decisive victory. The Egyptians would certainly have been pursued into their own country had not Nebuchadnezzar been called home by the death of his father. Necho agreed to relinquish his claims to Syria and Palestine. The Biblical historian simply states the result: "And the king of Egypt did not come again out of his land, for the king of Babylon had taken all that belonged to the king of Egypt from the Brook of Egypt to the river Euphrates" (II Kings 24:7). Even when Jehoiakim, who had been placed on the throne of Judah by Necho, rebelled against Nebuchadnezzar (597 B.C.), Necho did not come to his aid. Although Jerusalem was despoiled and part of its population taken into exile, Necho reconciled himself to the situation. Necho turned his attention instead to the development of commerce and the defenses of Egypt. About 600 B.C., he began the construction of a canal which was to connect the eastern arm of the Nile River with the Red Sea. Herodotus states that one hundred and twenty thousand men perished during the construction of the canal, and that Necho stopped the work when warned by an oracle that his canal would benefit the barbarian (i.e., foreigner) rather than the Egyptian.[1] Diodorus, on the other hand, tells us that Necho abandoned his project because he was told by his engineers that the Red Sea was higher than the Delta, and the canal would flood the entire Delta region.[2]

The canal left the Pelusiac branch of the Nile a short distance north of Bubastis. It circled eastward to Lake Timsah, and then turned southward parallel to the present Suez Canal along the west side of the Great Bitter Lake to the head of the Gulf of Suez. Its completion would have been of both commercial and military significance to Necho.

Necho dreamed of making Egypt a great sea power. He built an impressive fleet which sailed both the Red Sea and the Mediterranean. Necho also is remembered in the annals of exploration as the one who dispatched a crew of Phoenician mariners with instructions to sail around the African continent, known to the ancients as Libya. It took the Phoenicians three years to complete their mission.

In 593 B.C., Psammetichus II succeeded his father Necho as Pharaoh and continued his policies. Accompanied by a retinue of priests, he visited Phoenicia in 591 B.C. The trip was purely religious in motivation, however, for we are told that he brought along a votive wreath which was probably placed at the ancient Egyptian shrine at Byblos. No attempt was made to challenge the Babylonians in Syria. Instead he headed southward into lower Nubia and sent a body of troops as far as Abu Simbel, where they left a Greek inscription on one of the colossi of Ramesses II in front of his great temple there. The results of this campaign were not lasting, for we know that lower Nubia was not incorporated into Egypt.

Psammetichus was dependent on his Greek mercenaries, and seems to have been a great admirer of Greek culture. We are even told that the Eleans sent a deputation to ask his judgment

---

1. Herodotus, *Histories,* II, 158.
2. Diodorus, I, 33.9

as to the fairness of their administration of the Olympic Games. The native Egyptians tended to resent the preference which their ruler gave to the foreigners.

When Pharaoh Apries (Biblical Hophra) came to the throne in 588 B.C. he determined to challenge Nebuchadnezzar's control over Syria and Palestine. H. R. Hall calls him, "a headstrong and unwise person with neither the political wisdom of the elder Psammetichus nor the ordered energy of a Necho." He was, Hall continues, "The typical young king of the ancient world, full of energy, without the sagacity or cunning of his seniors and liable to be supported in foolish courses by an ignorant public opinion . . . largely of priestly inspiration."[3]

He found willing allies in Moab and Ammon. Zedekiah of Judah, although vacillating at times, decided to back the pro-Egyptian party in his court, and a major revolt against Nebuchadnezzar appeared imminent.

Apries, however, made the mistake of attacking his potential allies, the Phoenician cities of Tyre and Sidon. After a victorious naval engagement against the Tyrians, they yielded, and soon the Phoenician cities were all subject to him. Nebuchadnezzar, however, encamped at Riblah, on the Orontes River, taking no immediate steps against the Egyptians. Instead he turned his attention southward and besieged Jerusalem. The pro-Egyptian party there had expected Egyptian aid in such an emergency, but Egypt proved to be a broken reed.

In the summer of 588 B.C. an Egyptian army did march to challenge Nebuchadnezzar, and the siege of Jerusalem was temporarily lifted. Egypt, however, was no match for the Babylonian forces. The Egyptians under Apries were driven back, and the siege of Jerusalem continued until the city fell to Nebuchadnezzar (587 B.C.).

Things were not all easy for Nebuchadnezzar, however. Tyre was able to hold out against him until 574 B.C.

It was during the reign of Apries that the Jews were taken into Exile. Many Jews were able to escape southward into Egypt where they were permitted to settle in colonies of their own. Some journeyed as far as to Elephantine Island, at the first cataract of the Nile. The reign of Apries was a prosperous one, although he did have troubles keeping his troops content. On one occasion the Libyans, Greeks, and Syrians of his army

---

3. *The Cambridge Ancient History,* III, p. 502.

attempted to migrate to Nubia. They were dissuaded, however, by the governor of Aswan, and punished by Apries.

More serious difficulties developed when Greek settlers at Cyrene began to encroach on the territory of Libya, which lay between Cyrene and Egypt. The Libyans appealed to Apries who sent a force of Egyptians to aid them. He could not use Greek mercenaries against the Greeks of Cyrene. The Egyptian forces were almost annihilated by the Greeks of Cyrene and they became bitter against Apries. The Pharaoh tried to conciliate them by sending a member of the royal household, Ahmose, or Amasis as Herodotus designates him, to bring the rebels into submission. Amasis betrayed Apries by so manipulating the situation that the disaffected Egyptian soldiers proclaimed him king. A period of indecision and warfare ensued. After a brief co-regency, during which Apries took a subordinate position to Amasis, warfare broke out. The Greek mercenaries supported Apries but Amasis was supported by the native Egyptians. Apries died as a fugitive while resting in one of his few remaining boats. Amasis gave him an honorable burial, and secured for himself the throne of Egypt which he occupied until 525 B.C.

The forty-four year reign of Amasis saw no violent changes in Egyptian life, but the drift toward a Greek-oriented society continued. Nebuchadnezzar's armies approached the Egyptian Delta in 568 B.C., but details of his invasion are not known. A Babylonian text reads: ". . . in the 37th year, Nebuchadnezzar king of Babylon marched against Egypt (Mi-sir) to deliver a battle. (Ama)-sis of Egypt called up his army from the town of *Putu-Yaman.. . ."*[4] *Putu-Yaman* or *Putu-Javan* was probably the name of the Ionian city from which Amasis was able to summon mercenaries. Nebuchadnezzar did not conquer Egypt, but the campaign did force Amasis to renounce any plans for the conquest of Syria and Palestine.

Under Amasis, the Greek merchants were permitted to trade in only one city in the western Delta. Naucratis, on the Canopic Branch of the Nile, became both the home and market place of the Greeks and the most important commercial city of Egypt. Foreigners were forced to leave Daphne (Tahpanhes) and Migdol in 564 B.C. The Jews probably joined other of their people in upper Egypt, although some may have returned to Palestine.

---

4. A. Leo Oppenheim, "Babylonian and Assyrian Historical Texts," in James Pritchard, *Ancient Near Eastern Texts*, p. 308.

Amasis kept on very friendly terms with the Greeks, even marrying a Cyrenaean Greek, Ladice. Greek mercenaries served as a palace guard at Memphis where they could be depended upon to guarantee Amasis' personal safety in the event of revolt. He contributed toward the erection of Greek temples and had warm friendships with such Greek rulers as Polycrates of Samos.

As a wise statesman, Amasis did not neglect his own people. Additions were made to the temples at Sais and Memphis. Herodotus speaks of him in glowing terms:

> It is said that in the reign of Amasis, Egypt attained to its greatest prosperity, in respect of what the river did for the land and the land for its people: and that the whole sum of inhabited cities in the country was twenty thousand. It was Amasis also who made the law that every Egyptian should yearly declare his means of livelihood to the ruler of his province, and, failing so to do or to prove that he had a just way of life, be punished with death. Solon the Athenian got this law from Egypt and established it among his people; may they ever keep it! for it is a perfect law.[5]

Amasis did not, of course, rule an empire which could be compared with that of the ancient Pharaohs. His was an Egypt which was soon to lose its distinctive culture and its very independence. Although Nebuchadnezzar did not conquer Egypt, and Babylon itself fell to the Persians in 539 B.C., Egypt would not stand long before the powerful forces which were developing in the East. Cambyses, the son and heir of Cyrus the Persian, was to conquer Egypt in 525 B.C. — just months after the death of Amasis.

---

5. Herodotus, *Histories*, II, 177.

4

JEREMIAH OF JERUSALEM

Much of our knowledge of the events preceding the capture of Jerusalem comes from the Book of Jeremiah. The prophecies of Jeremiah were largely unheeded by the generation which heard them but, faithfully preserved by the scribe Baruch, they became a source of hope and challenge to subsequent generations.

Jeremiah was a native of Anathoth, a city in Benjamin near the northern boundary of Jerusalem. Anathoth had been allotted to the priests of the line of Ithamar, the youngest son of Aaron. Eli, a descendant of Ithamar, had served as priest at Shiloh. A later descendant, Abiathar, supported David's son Adonijah in his bid for the throne. When Solomon succeeded in thwarting the plans of Adonijah, Abiathar was expelled and Zadok, a priest of the family of Eleazar, Aaron's oldest son, replaced him. In expelling Abiathar, Solomon said, "Go to Anathoth, to your estate" (I Kings 2:26).

The opening words of the Book of Jeremiah identify the prophet as "of the priests who were in Anathoth." There is no hint, however, that he ever functioned as a priest. While quite young (Jer. 1:6) he was called to the prophetic office. Anathoth was but three miles northeast of Jerusalem and it is probable that Jeremiah continued to live in his home town during the early years of his ministry. Later his townsmen expressed active hostility (Jer. 11:21; 12:6) and the prophet moved into Jerusalem.

Jeremiah's call to a prophetic ministry came during the reign of Josiah. This was the last great period of spiritual revival in the history of Judah. Josiah called his people back to God and obedience to the Law which had long been forgotten. It is probable that Jeremiah himself joined in this ministry, perhaps carrying the reform message to Anathoth. With the

death of Josiah on the battlefield of Megiddo, the old idolatry
became more firmly entrenched than ever and Jeremiah was to
spend years of loneliness as he attempted to hold forth God's
message to a restless and rebellious people.

The terms of Jeremiah's call were a foreshadowing of the
nature of his ministry:

> Behold, I have put my words in your mouth.
> See, I have set you this day over nations and over kingdoms,
> to pluck up and to break down,
> to destroy and to overthrow,
> to build and to plant (Jer. 1:9-10).

There was a strong negative side to Jeremiah's work. He was
to stand against prophets, priests, kings, and people in cham-
pioning the cause of the Lord. He would be considered a traitor
for predicting defeat at the hand of Judah's enemy, Babylon.
Yet there was a building and planting which his ministry ac-
complished. After the death of Jeremiah, his word found a
response in the hearts of a people chastened through exile, yet
conscious that their God had not utterly forsaken them.

Jehoiakim came to the throne of Judah as a vassal of Egypt.
Jeremiah insisted that the only hope for Judah was in the
recognition of the Babylonian power. Thus the policy of the
prophet was diametrically opposed to that of the king. Most
of the religious leaders of Judah were sympathetic with Jehoiakim. They assured their fellow-countrymen that Nebuchadnezzar would do them no harm. Had not God delivered Jerusalem from Sennacherib during the days of Hezekiah and
Isaiah? The Holy City was inviolable. God would never allow
the heathen to desecrate Jerusalem!

These sentiments stirred Jeremiah to the point where he
went to the gate of the Sanctuary and delivered his famous
Temple Address. He called upon the people to turn from their
evil ways and warned them against false prophets who cried
out, "This is the Temple of the Lord, the Temple of the Lord,
the Temple of the Lord" (Jer. 7:4). Their attitude reduced the
God of Israel to the level of the gods of the heathen who were
unconcerned with morality. God could save His people from
their enemies, but He also could deliver His people into the
hands of their enemies for chastisement. Jeremiah drew upon
history: "Go now to my place which was in Shiloh, where I
made my name dwell at first, and see what I did to it for the
wickedness of my people Israel" (Jer. 7:12). Shiloh had been a
sanctuary in the days of Eli and Samuel, but it was destroyed
in the wars with the "uncircumcised Philistine." The Northern

Kingdom, the "offspring of Ephraim" (Jer. 7:15) had gone into captivity a little more than a century before Jeremiah's ministry. They had resisted the ministries of Hosea, Amos, and others who called them back to God. Jeremiah insisted that there was no room for complacency on the part of idolatrous Judah. False prophets cry "Peace, peace," but there is no peace (Jer. 8:11). Judgment is at hand!

Jeremiah's Temple Address produced an immediate and hostile response from his audience. The priests and prophets said to the princes and people, "This man deserves the sentence of death, because he has prophesied against this city, as you have heard with your own ears" (Jer. 26:11). Prophets were expected to predict good things and build up the morale of the people. Jeremiah dared to do the opposite.

The prophet was spared, however, when certain of the elders reminded the people of the words of Micah who had prophesied in the days of Hezekiah saying: "Zion shall be plowed as a field; Jerusalem shall become a heap of ruins, and the mountain of the house a wooded height" (Jer. 26:18; cf. Micah 3:12). The words proved timely. Jeremiah was not put to death. Another prophet, Uriah the son of Shemaiah, had prophesied against Jerusalem and was killed for his insolence. He had found temporary asylum in Egypt, but Jehoiakim sent for him and killed him (Jer. 26:20-24).

During the fourth year of Jehoiakim, Jeremiah was directed by God to gather together the prophecies which he had delivered during a ministry which had lasted about twenty-three years. Jeremiah dictated the messages to his scribe Baruch, who recorded them on a scroll. Subsequently, when the people were gathered at the Temple to observe a fast decreed by Jehoiakim, Baruch took his book and read it "at the entry of the New Gate of the Lord's house" (Jer. 36:10). Some of the princes wanted the king to hear these prophecies. They questioned Baruch concerning them, and then had the scroll read before Jehoiakim. The king showed his contempt for Jeremiah and his message by burning the scroll in the fire of his brazier (Jer. 36:1-22).

Jeremiah and Baruch would certainly have been killed had they not been protected by friendly princes who urged them to find a secret hiding-place (Jer. 36:19). When word reached them of the destruction of the first scroll, Jeremiah dictated another to which "Many similar words" were added (Jer. 36:32). This may be considered the earliest edition of what became our Book of Jeremiah.

Within three months after Jehoiachin succeeded his father Jehoiakim to the throne of Judah, Nebuchadnezzar was besieging the city of Jerusalem (cf. Jer. 22:18-30). The Egyptians were powerless to interfere, and the young king was taken into exile by the Babylonians. Jerusalem was not destroyed, but tribute was imposed upon its rulers and ten thousand of its inhabitants went into exile (II Kings 24:14).

When Zedekiah was confirmed on the throne of Judah by Nebuchadnezzar, the prophecies of Jeremiah and the policy which he endorsed should have gained a respectful hearing. Indeed we do read of Zedekiah seeking counsel of the prophet (Jer. 37:16-21). The king was a confused man, however. The pro-Egyptian party was not dead, and its prophets declared that Jehoiachin and the exiles would be back from Babylon within two years (Jer. 28:1-5).

Jeremiah sought to show the error of the false prophets, and insisted that the exiles would remain in Babylon for seventy years (Jer. 29:10). He went so far as to address a letter to them, urging them to build homes, marry, and raise families in their new surroundings (Jer. 29:1-7). He assured them that God would ultimately bring them back, but urged them to seek the welfare of the city in which they would dwell until that distant day should arrive (Jer. 29:7).

During the eleven year reign of Zedekiah, Jeremiah continued to announce the impending judgment which would fall upon Israel. His gloomy predictions were relieved only by the message that God would not cast off His people forever. There were no violent persecutions of the prophet during the early years of Zedekiah's reign. As things reached a climax, however, Jeremiah could not escape the antagonism of his people. Determined to rebel against Nebuchadnezzar, the rulers of Jerusalem could not permit Jeremiah to prophesy Babylonian victory. The prophet was arrested while journeying to Benjamin, charged with being a deserter, and cast into the common prison. There he remained "many days" (Jer. 37:16). Zedekiah, who both respected and feared Jeremiah, later ordered the prophet removed to the court of the guard (Jer. 37:21), evidently a much more pleasant place of confinement. The king actually sought the advice of Jeremiah from time to time, but the message he received was unvarying: "You shall be delivered into the hand of the king of Babylon" (Jer. 37:17).

The prophet's dark forebodings and the approach of Nebuchadnezzar's armies, threw all Jerusalem into turmoil. The princes could delay no longer. They approached Zedekiah with the demand: "Let this man be put to death, for he is weakening the hands of the soldiers who are left in this city, and the hands of all the people, by speaking such words to them. For this man is not seeking the welfare of this people, but their harm" (Jer. 38:4).

The nobles, armed with the royal mandate, entered the court of the prison and took Jeremiah, casting him into a cistern which was so deep that he had to be let down by ropes (Jer. 37:6). There he sank into the mire and would have died but for an Ethiopian eunuch, Ebed-melech, who pleaded with the king on Jeremiah's behalf, and secured an order for his release. Ebed-melech and three companions, armed with ropes and old rags, went to the cistern and drew out the prophet. Jeremiah remained in the court of the guard until released by Nebuchadnezzar after the fall of Jerusalem.

The imprisonment of Jeremiah must have continued for more than a year. During this time the prophet continued to declare the word of God and depict events in the immediate and the more remote future. We hear his triumphant assurance:

> In this place of which you say, "It is a waste without man or beast," in the cities of Judah and the streets of Jerusalem that are desolate, without man or inhabitant or beast, there shall be heard again the voice of mirth and the voice of gladness, the voice of the bridegroom and the voice of the bride.... For I will restore the fortunes of the land as at the first, says the Lord (Jer. 33:10-11).

Jeremiah demonstrated his faith in deed as well as word. Hanameel, his uncle's son, offered to sell the prophet a plot of ground in Anathoth. Jeremiah knew that Jerusalem would soon be in Babylonian control, and Nebuchadnezzar's armies may already have reached Anathoth. Yet Jeremiah had implicit faith in God's promises, and knew that the land would one day return to Israelite control. After proper legal formalities were concluded, Jeremiah weighed out the seventeen shekels of silver which he agreed to pay for the property and took possession. He then turned the deed over to Baruch with the injunction, "Take these deeds, both this sealed deed of purchase and this open deed, and put them in an earthen vessel that they may last for a long time" (Jer. 32:14).

The fall of Jerusalem vindicated the ministry of Jeremiah, but it certainly brought him no joy. The beautiful palace was in ruins. The Temple, built by Solomon in an era during which the glories of Jerusalem were known throughout the East, was but rubble. The wavering Zedekiah, who from time to time had

sought counsel of Jeremiah, was blinded, chained, and taken as
a trophy of war to Babylon. The king's sons and the nobles had
been slain.

Jeremiah was not deported, however. He, with the remnants
of the Judaeans, remained in Palestine where a loyal Israelite,
Gedaliah, was appointed by Nebuchadnezzar to serve as governor
at Mizpah. A pretender, Ishmael, with Ammonite support, murdered Gedaliah and attempted to set up an independent government. In spite of the warnings of Jeremiah, the remnant of the
Judaeans determined to flee to Egypt to escape the wrath of
Nebuchadnezzar which would surely be felt after the murder of
the governor he had appointed. Jeremiah and his scribe, Baruch,
were forced to journey to Egypt along with the men of Judah
who hoped to find a place of refuge there. In the Egyptian city
of Tahpanhes, Jeremiah uttered his last recorded prophecies
(Jer. 43:7).

Jeremiah has been called "the weeping prophet." Whether or
not he wrote the Book of Lamentations, the description is a fit-
ting one. Few men have been as lonely as he. From the purely
human viewpoint, Jeremiah's life was a failure. His people continued in the sins which he denounced. They could not see the
will of God in submission to the power of Babylon as he demanded, and the pro-Egyptian party gained the ear of both
Jehoiakim and Zedekiah. A fictionalized ending of the story of
Jeremiah tells us that he was released from Egypt and spent his
last years in Babylon. The wish seems to be father to the thought,
however. Ironically the Scripture leaves him in Egypt — the
source of promised help which never came to Judah, and the nation whose promises were never taken seriously by Jeremiah.

The life span of Jeremiah encompassed the years from the last
great revival under Josiah, to the defeat of his country and the
desecration of its Temple. Jeremiah did more than weep, however. He saw through his tears the promise of a bright future
when God would restore Zion and write a new covenant upon
the hearts of His people. Plagued by weak and idolatrous kings,
Jeremiah looked to the day when God would "raise up for David
a righteous Branch" who would "execute justice and righteousness in the land" (Jer. 23:5).

5

THE LACHISH LETTERS

The prophecies of Jeremiah give us a vivid picture of life in Jerusalem during the difficult years before the city fell to Nebuchadnezzar. Thanks to the work of J. L. Starkey, the British archaeologist who excavated Tell ed-Duweir, Biblical Lachish, we now have a description of life outside Jerusalem during the time of the Babylonian invasion.

In 1935 Starkey, while directing the Wellcome-Marston Research Expedition, came upon a small guardroom adjoining the outer gate of Lachish. There, buried in a layer of charcoal and ashes, he found sixteen broken pieces of pottery which contained writing in the Old Hebrew, or Phoenician script. Two other pieces were found nearby and three additional pieces were discovered in 1938, one on the roadway and two in a room near the palace.

These inscribed potsherds, technically known as ostraca, were for the most part letters written by the scribes of Hoshaiah, evidently an Israelite soldier stationed at a military outpost. The messages were addressed to Yaosh, the commanding officer at Lachish. They are written in a terse, telegraphic style, and the modern reader has difficulty reconstructing the exact circumstances during which they were written. Mr. Starkey noted that the ostraca which were arbitrarily numbered II, VI, VII, VIII, and XVIII are all pieces of the same pot, indicating that they were written at about the same time. Professor Harry Torcyner, who edited the texts for publication, noted similarities in handwriting between these letters and other potsherds from a different source. The numbers assigned to the ostraca provide a convenient means of reference, but they have no significance. Some of the ostraca are merely lists of names which were meaningful to the original writer and recipient, but serve only to illustrate Israelite names of the time for the modern student. Although

The Mound of Lachish. Thirty miles southwest of Jerusalem on the main road from central Palestine to Egypt was the fortified city of Lachish, modern Tell ed-Duweir. J. L. Starkey excavated the site for the Wellcome-Marston Archaeological Expedition from 1933 to 1938.

Photo courtesy of the Trustees of the late Sir Henry Wellcome.

Judaean Lachish. Excavations at Tell ed-Duweir indicate that Lachish was one of the largest occupied sites in ancient Palestine. It was one of the last cities to fall to Nebuchadnezzar (cf. Jer. 34:7). Reconstruction by H. H. McWilliams, courtesy the Trustees of the late Sir Henry Wellcome.

they are not to be identified with the Biblical characters who
bore the same names, it is of interest that the first Lachish letter
mentions a Yirmiyahu, or Jeremiah, and a Mattanyahu (Mattaniah), the name of Zedekiah before Nebuchadnezzar appointed
him king.

The letters make use of conventional expressions. A flowery
salutation may open the letter, and the writer often speaks of
himself in abject humility as a dog (cf. II Sam. 9:8). Similar expressions are used in the Amarna Letters (14th century B.C.) in
which a vassal deprecates himself in addressing his overlord.

The second of the Lachish Ostraca illustrates these conventions.
It reads:

> To my lord, Yaosh: May Yahweh cause my lord to hear tidings of peace
> this very day, this very day! Who is thy servant (but) a dog that my lord
> hath remembered his servant? May Yahweh afflict those who report an
> (evil) rumor about which thou art not informed!

Evidently things were not going well for the Judaeans. The
writer of the letter feared that an evil report had reached Yaosh.
He expresses a desire that the commander will hear tidings of
peace, but we know that this did not take place.

The longest of the ostraca is the third. It is a letter from Hoshaiah to Yaosh:

> Thy servant Hoshaiah hath sent to inform my lord Yaosh: May Yahweh
> cause my lord to hear tidings of peace! And now thou hast sent a letter,
> but my lord did not enlighten thy servant concerning the letter which
> thou didst send to thy servant yesterday evening, though the heart of thy
> servant hath been sick since thou didst write to thy servant. And as for
> what my lord said, "Dost thou not understand? — call a scribe!" as
> Yahweh liveth no one hath ever undertaken to call a scribe for me; and
> as for any scribe who might have come to me, truly I did not call him
> nor would I give anything at all for him!
> And it hath been reported to thy servant, saying, "The commander
> of the host, Coniah son of Elnathan, hath come down in order to go into
> Egypt; and unto Hodaviah son of Ahijah and his men that he sent to
> obtain ... from him."
> And as for the letter of Tobiah, servant of the king, which came to
> Shallum son of Jaddua through the prophet, saying "Beware!" thy servant
> hath sent it to my lord.

Evidently Hoshaiah had been scolded for disregarding orders
contained in an earlier letter. Some think that he disclosed the
contents of a secret communication. He insisted that he had not
wilfully disobeyed. The letter speaks of a trip to Egypt made by a
man named Coniah, son of Elnathan. The Judaean kings looked
to Egypt for help during the time of their war with Babylon.
Egypt, fearful of the growing power of Babylon, and anxious to
build an empire for herself, gladly supported any movement in
Judah that sought to resist Nebuchadnezzar. Pharaoh Psammeti-

chus II sent a force to relieve besieged Jerusalem (Jer. 37:15), but the Babylonians soon dispersed them and resumed their siege.

Mention is also made of a prophet who had delivered a letter of warning to a man named Shallum. We cannot identify this prophet, but we know that there were many men who bore the title "prophet" during the years before the fall of Jerusalem. Letter 16 also speaks of a prophet and his name is known to have ended with the familiar -iah suffix. Some have suggested that he was the Uriah of Jeremiah 26:20-23, or even Jeremiah himself, but we have no real basis for such identifications. False prophets plagued Jeremiah and soothed the people with words of peace when Jeremiah assured them, "There is no peace."

Ostracon Four appears to have been written shortly before the fall of Lachish itself. It reads:

> May Yahweh cause my lord to hear this very day tidings of good! And now according to everything that my lord hath written, so hath thy servant done; I have written on the door according to all that my lord hath written to me. And with respect to what my lord hath written about the matter of Beth-haraphid, there is no one there.
>
> And as for Semachiah, Shemaiah hath taken him and brought him to the city. And as for thy servant, I am not sending anyone thither. (today (?), but I will send) tomorrow morning.
>
> And let (my lord) know that we are watching for the signals of Lachish, according to all the indications which my lord hath given, for we cannot see Azekah.

Writing "on the door" was tantamount to posting on the bulletin board for all to see. It will be remembered that Luther's famous theses were posted on the door of the Castle church at Wittenburg over two thousand years after the Lachish letters!

The last paragraph of the letter contained the sad news that the fire signals from Azekah could no longer be seen. This could mean but one thing. Azekah had fallen to the enemy. By 588 B.C. only three cities remained to the Judaeans — Azekah, Lachish, and Jerusalem (Jer. 34:6-7). Our letter must have been written that year. Azekah had fallen, but Lachish was still in Judaean hands. This situation did not last for long, however, for soon Lachish fell, then Jerusalem, and Judah as an independent political state lost its identity.

The Lachish correspondence tells us something of the military organization of the day. A system of signals had been devised and reports could normally be made from a distance. We read of these signals in Jeremiah 6:1 where the prophet cries out: "Blow the trumpet in Tekoa, and raise a signal on Beth-haccherem; for evil looms out of the north, and great destruction." Written reports were regularly sent to headquarters, and orders from headquarters were sent to the field commanders at military outposts.

Morale was a problem during Judah's last days. Jeremiah was threatened with death for discouraging the people with his prophecies of doom (Jer. 38:4). The sixth ostracon reflects a lowering of morale:

> To my lord Yaosh: may Yahweh cause my lord to see this season in good health! Who is thy servant (but) a dog that my lord hath sent the letter of the king and the letters of the princes saying, "Pray, read them!" And behold the words of the princes are not good, (but) to weaken our hands (and to sla)cken the hands of the m (en who are informed about them (...And now) my lord, wilt thou not write to them saying, "Why do ye thus (even) in Jerusalem? Behold unto the king and unto (his house) are ye doing this thing!" (And,) as Yahweh thy God liveth, truly since thy servant read the letters there hath been no (peace) for (thy ser)vant...

Only one of the texts, Ostracon Number 20, is dated. It begins "In the ninth year." That was the year during which Nebuchadnezzar invaded Judah to put down Zedekiah's revolt (II Kings 25:1). Two years later (July, 587 B.C.) during the eleventh year of Zedekiah, the walls of Jerusalem were breached and the city fell. The inscribed potsherds from Lachish give us a picture of life during those difficult years. Jeremiah was prophesying within Jerusalem. His prophecies, and the cryptic notes of Judaean field commanders found by Starkey at Lachish, give us a first hand account of life both within and outside Jerusalem during the months before the last stronghold of Judah fell to Babylon.

Dr. W. F. Albright, writing about the Lachish ostraca, observes,

> In these letters we find ourselves in exactly the age of Jeremiah, with social and political connotations agreeing perfectly with the picture drawn in the book that bears his name.[1]

---

1. "The Oldest Hebrew Letters," *Bulletin of the American Schools of Oriental Research,* Number 7 (April 1938), p. 17.

6

JUDAH DURING THE EXILIC PERIOD

With the destruction of Jerusalem, Judah ceased to exist as a sovereign state. Zedekiah died shortly after being taken to Babylon. Jehoiachin, although looked upon as the legitimate king, had no reasonable hope of returning to his land.

The Babylonians established a military government for Judah with headquarters at Mizpah, about eight miles north of Jerusalem. A Judaean, Gedaliah, was named governor. Gedaliah was the son of Shaphan who had protected Jeremiah from the wrath of Jehoiakim and his nobles (Jer. 26:24). He would have been considered pro-Babylonian and thus suitable for an appointment which must be sympathetic to Babylonian rule. After Jerusalem fell to Nebuchadnezzar, the Babylonian military officers asked Gedaliah to look after the safety of Jeremiah (Jer. 39:11-14).

Gedaliah formed a center around which the Judaeans who had not been taken into exile might gather. Those who had fled to Edom, Moab, and Ammon trickled back. Gedaliah counseled loyalty to Nebuchadnezzar: "Dwell in the land, and serve the king of Babylon, and it shall be well with you" (Jer. 40:9). Evidently a degree of prosperity ensued for "they gathered wine and summer fruits in great abundance" (Jer. 40:12).

In the ruins of Mizpah (Tell en-Nasbeh) a seal was found bearing the identifying inscription "To Jaazaniah, servant of the king." Jaazaniah was one of the officials associated with Gedaliah (II Kings 25:23; Jer. 40:8). A seal impression found among the ruins of Lachish bears the inscription, "To Gedaliah who is over the house."

George Ernest Wright suggests that Gedaliah had served as one of the last prime ministers of Judah. He notes that the seal found at Lachish must antedate the destruction of the city by Nebuchadnezzar's armies. The words "who is over the house" suggest the office of prime minister. Not only was Gedaliah's

father a high official in his own right (Jer. 26:24), but his grand-
father, Shaphan, had served Josiah as Scribe, or Secretary of State
(II Kings 22:3, 8-12).[1]

The wise rule of Gedaliah at Mizpah came to a violent end.
Ishmael, a man whose royal blood encouraged him to seek the
throne for himself (Jer. 41:1; II Kings 25:25), had fled to Ammon
during the siege of Jerusalem. He found a ready ally in Baalis,
the king of Ammon. Learning that Gedaliah was governor of the
remnant of the Judaeans at Mizpah, Ishmael went there with a
band of ten men and treacherously killed Gedaliah. Gedaliah
had been warned about the plot, but he refused to believe the
evil report concerning Ishmael (Jer. 40:16).

In addition to Gedaliah, Ishmael killed eighty men who had
come to worship at the shrine at Mizpah (Jer. 41:4-7), and took
captive the others who had settled there, intending to bring them
to Ammon (Jer. 41:10). At Gibeon, Ishmael was challenged by
the forces of the loyal Judaean, Johanan the son of Kareah. Although Ishmael escaped and presumably reached Ammon, his
captives were freed and then, contrary to the counsel of Jeremiah, fled southward to Egypt.

The history of Judah between the destruction of Jerusalem
(587 B.C.) and the return of the first group of exiles following the decree of Cyrus (536 B.C.) is largely a blank. The
province of Judah, which Gedaliah had ruled, was abolished,
and its territory incorporated into the neighboring province
of Samaria. Some of the older Biblical scholars held that
there was no drastic break in the continuity of life in Judah
following Nebuchadnezzar's destruction of Jerusalem. It was assumed that natives returned to their homes and life continued
without serious interruption. According to these scholars, the
exile involved only a few nobles, and the accounts in Kings,
Ezekiel, and Ezra-Nehemiah are grossly exaggerated.

Archaeology, however, has shown a decisive break in Palestinian life during the years following 587 B.C. No town in Judah
was continually occupied throughout the exilic period. While
there was a complete break in the history of Judah, this was not
true of the area north or south of the Judaean border. Bethel
and the Samaritan cities were not destroyed and the towns of the
Negeb were left undisturbed. Discussing the excavation of towns
and fortresses in Judah, Albright says,

---

1. *Biblical Archaeology*, p. 178.

The results are uniform and conclusive: many towns were destroyed at the beginning of the sixth century B.C. and never again occupied; others were destroyed at that time and partly occupied at some later date; still others were destroyed and reoccupied after a long period of abandonment, marked by a sharp change of stratum and by intervening indications of use for non-urban purposes. There is not a single known case where a town of Judah proper was continuously occupied through the exilic period. Just to point the contrast, Bethel, which lay just outside the northern boundary of Judah in pre-exilic times, was not destroyed at that time, but was continuously occupied down into the latter part of the sixth century.[2]

Among the towns of Judaea which were destroyed and never rebuilt were Beth-shemesh and Tell Beit Mirsim (Kirjath-sepher). Excavators found that there were some periods when sites were not in use as they studied layers which date earlier than the sixth century B.C. It was only during the period of the Babylonian conquest of Judah that large numbers of sites permanently ceased to be occupied.

Unlike the Assyrians, who repopulated the Northern Kingdom after its fall in 722 B.C. (II Kings 17:24), the Babylonians did not make it a policy to repopulate areas from which captives had been taken. Instead the land was gradually occupied by neighboring tribes — Edomites and Arabians pressing in from the south and Ammonites and other tribes from east of the Jordan crossing the river to occupy such territory as they could claim. Before the return of exiles from Babylonia, Judah was dominated by alien peoples with those descendants of the former Jewish population that had not been deported. The area occupied by the Jews who returned following the decree of Cyrus was not much more than Jerusalem and its suburbs.

The Jews who were left in Palestine during the period of the Exile had much in common with their Samaritan neighbors to the north. Both groups worshiped the same God, Yahweh, and both accepted the Mosaic Law as Holy Writ. The syncretism which marked the earliest Samaritans (II Kings 17:33) seems to have disappeared in later Samaritan thinking. Their distinctive faith was in the sanctity of Mount Gerizim as the Temple site (John 4:20). This, however, was not implemented until the Sanctuary was built on Mount Gerizim in post-exilic times.[3]

Judging by the problems faced by reformers of a later day the Jews and Samaritans of Palestine must have gotten along quite well together. Intermarriage became quite common, for it was a serious problem in the days of Ezra and Nehemiah (cf. Ezra

---

2. *The Archaeology of Palestine,* pp. 141-142.
3. See p. 117.

10:18-44; Neh. 13:23-28). Sanballat, the governor of Samaria, gave his daughter in marriage to a grandson of the High Priest Eliashib, much to the dismay of Nehemiah (Neh. 13:28). It was the Jews who returned from exile who insisted on strict separation from the Samaritans and other non-Jewish peoples of Palestine.

For fifty years after the destruction of Jerusalem, Judah was left to its own devices. While exiles in Babylon dreamed of returning to their Palestinian homes, the inhabitants of Judah — Jews, and non-Jews — had adjusted to a new mode of life. It is understandable that Samaritans should resent the return of exiles from Babylon and that some Jews would desire to keep ties of friendship with them.

7

THE CRISIS OF EXILE

Of the many crises which Israel had experienced, none was more fraught with danger than the Babylonian Exile. The persecutions in Egypt had welded the tribes into a unified people during the time of Moses. The Philistine threat brought about the demand for a king and national solidarity in the days of the later Judges. The disruption of the kingdom following the death of Solomon was followed by a period of political weakness and civil war, but the Davidic throne was preserved in Judah even during periods of apostasy.

The Exile, however, was an event to challenge the faith of the most orthodox Jew. The Lord of hosts who had delivered Jericho into Joshua's hand had gone down in defeat — or so it seemed. Ancient peoples thought of battles among the nations as reflecting a parallel warfare among the gods. The nation with the strongest god would be expected to win. When Jerusalem was destroyed it would have been natural to conclude that Marduk, the god of Babylon, had proved himself stronger than the God of Israel. The very vessels from the Lord's house in Jerusalem became trophies of victory in Marduk's shrine in Babylon.

Gods were usually associated with the territory of the people who worshiped them. Yahweh, the God of Israel, would be reckoned as the God of a land which had been stripped of its population. Years before the Exile, Ben-hadad of Damascus had shown that he thought of Israel's god in geographical terms when he concluded, "Their gods are gods of the hills, and so they were stronger than we; but let us fight against them in the plain, and surely we shall be stronger than they" (I Kings 20:23).

Naaman, the Aramaean captain, showed the same feeling toward Israel's God, although he wished to become a worshiper of Yahweh when he returned to his Aramaean home. Through the instrumentality of Elisha, Naaman had been cured of leprosy.

Faced with the problem that Rimmon was the god who was worshiped in his native Damascus, Naaman devised a rather unor-
thodox solution. He made a simple request: ". . . let there be
given to your servant two mules' burden of earth; for henceforth
your servant will not offer burnt offering or sacrifices to any god
but Yahweh" (II Kings 5:5). He could bring to Damascus some
of the land where Yahweh was worshiped!

One of the great burdens of the prophetic writers of the exilic
period was the proneness of the people to entertain localized
views of Israel's god. Yahweh was the God of all the earth! He
was the creator, not of Israel alone, but of all mankind. Although banished from the land which He had given to the
fathers and, later, to Joshua, Israel must see that her God was
not a weakling, but One whose purposes were carried out even
in the moment of the defeat of His people. The second verse of
the Book of Daniel contains the startling assertion: "The Lord
gave Jehoiakim, king of Judah, into his [Nebuchadnezzar's]
hand, with some of the vessels of the house of God." Only as the
faithful of Israel could discern the significance of such words
could the nation survive the Exile.

Power and holiness were important attributes of Israel's God.
In the crisis of the Babylonian threat, these attributes might
seem to involve an impasse. If the armies of Nebuchadnezzar
should actually destroy Jerusalem and its Temple, Israel's God
would appear to be weak in not protecting His people. God's
name, or reputation, seemed to be at stake. The Psalmist cried
out, "For thy name's sake, O Lord, preserve my life!" (Psalm
143:11). God is concerned about His name. He desired that his
Name be reverenced not alone in Israel but also among the nations.

Yet God revealed Himself both in His Word and in His works
as a holy God. What could be gained in delivering Israel from
the pagan Babylonian if pagan elements were permitted to continue in Israel? Jeremiah accused his countrymen of worshiping
as many gods as Judah had cities (Jer. 11:13). Even Babylon was
no more idolatrous than that. God had given solemn warning
in His Law:

> You shall remember Yahweh your God, for it is he who gives you
> power to get wealth; that he may confirm his covenant which he swore
> to your fathers, as at this day. And if you forget Yahweh your god and
> go after other gods and serve them and worship them, I solemnly warn
> you this day that you shall surely perish. Like the nations that Yahweh
> makes to perish before you, so shall you perish, because you would not
> obey the voice of Yahweh your God (Deut. 8:18-20).

This solemn warning might well raise the question of Israel's divine election, and the covenants which God had made with David. Through Nathan, the prophet, God said, "I will appoint a place for my people Israel, and will plant them, that they may dwell in their own place, and be disturbed no more; and violent men shall afflict them no more . . . and I will give you rest from all your enemies . . . " (II Sam. 7:10-11). Addressing David, Nathan continued: "And your house and your kingdom shall be made sure forever before me; your throne shall be established for ever" (II Sam. 7:16).

With the disruption of the kingdom following Solomon's death and the checkered history of Israel and Judah, the significance of these words must often have been missed. Yet they were never forgotten. When the armies of the Assyrian king, Sennacherib, were at the gates of Jerusalem, Hezekiah was understandably worried. The prophet Isaiah assured him that the city was inviolable, quoting an oracle from the Lord: "I will defend this city to save it for my own sake and for the sake of my servant David" (II Kings 19:34). Sennacherib was forced to lift his siege. The power of Israel's God was demonstrated. Hezekiah, David's "son" (i.e., descendant) was left secure on the throne. God had not forgotten His covenant with David.

Hezekiah's godly reign was followed by apostasy, however. Except for the significant revival during the reign of Josiah, Judah's subsequent history was marked by idolatry and religious formality devoid of spiritual meaning. The populace took their spiritual blessings for granted and assumed that they were safe because of their favored position as a "chosen people."

In Jeremiah's day false prophets were confidently proclaiming, "This is the Temple of the Lord, the Temple of the Lord, the Temple of the Lord" (Jer. 7:4). They assumed that the Babylonian could not touch it because of its sacred associations, but Jeremiah warned, "This house shall be like Shiloh, and this city shall be desolate, without inhabitant" (Jer. 25:9).

While insisting that Jerusalem would be destroyed and its people taken into exile, Jeremiah was not unmindful of the covenant between God and His people. In holiness, God would deliver His people to their enemies, but in power He would bring them back to their own land. Through the affliction of captivity, Israel would be prepared for a brighter future: "There is hope for your future, says the Lord, and your children shall come back to their own country" (Jer. 31:17).

Hope, however, was conditioned on a change of heart. Idolatry is an offense to God, and His people can expect no blessing as long as they continue in rebellion against Him. Jeremiah assured the exiles, in an oracle of God, "You will seek me and find me; when you seek me with all your heart, I will be found by you, says the Lord, and I will restore your fortunes and gather you from all the nations and all the places where I have driven you, says the Lord, and I will bring you back to the place from which I sent you into exile" (Jer. 29:14).

In his letter to the exiles in Babylon, Jeremiah urged them to build houses, plant gardens, raise families, and seek to live normal lives in the land of their captivity. They were urged to seek the welfare of Babylon, for their own welfare would be contingent on the welfare of the land in which they lived. They were not to assume that the captivity would be permanent, however, for they were assured. "When seventy years are completed for Babylon, I will visit you, and I will fulfill to you my promise and bring you back to this place" (Jer. 29:10).

The words of Jeremiah were not appreciated by the generation in which he lived. It was easier to believe the prophets who cried out "Peace, Peace," and assured the people that all was well. These false prophets said that the people who had gone into captivity with Jehoiachin would be back within two years (cf. Jer. 28:1-4). Jeremiah was considered a defeatist if not an actual enemy of the people because he dared to assert that Israel's armies would go down in defeat before Nebuchadnezzar.

Yet Jeremiah prepared Israel for the crisis of the Exile. Events proved that his words were true. Trusting the words of false prophets, Israel went down in defeat. Jerusalem was destroyed and her people deported. Could God watch over his people in a strange land and bring them back? Those who had a lesser concept of Israel's God were destined to be absorbed among the gentiles and never heard from again. The remnant which believed in the power and the purposes of God, even in Babylon, formed the nucleus which one day was to return and rebuild the desolate cities of Judah.

8

LIFE AMONG THE EXILES

The Jews in Exile were permitted to form colonies in which their communal life could continue. The pious Jew wept when he remembered Zion. He felt that he could not sing the Lord's song in a strange land. In time, however, most of the Jews made adjustment to their Babylonian environment. They took to heart the counsel of Jeremiah and prepared for an exile of seventy years. The prophet had urged them to marry, build houses, plant vineyards, and in other ways adapt themselves to Babylonian life. Few who had left Jerusalem could expect to return. Most would spend their remaining days in the land of their exile, and it was incumbent on them to find a satisfactory life there.

We do not know anything about Tel-abib, the settlement in which Ezekiel ministered, except for the fact that it was on the river Chebar, an important canal located southeast of the city of Babylon. As a smaller community, Tel-abib would not possess the splendors of Babylon but life there would have its compensations. Country houses away from the larger cities were often set in gardens which were irrigated by the canals which controlled the flood waters of the Tigris and Euphrates rivers. These canals greatly increased the area of arable land in Babylonia.

Gardens were rectangular in shape, situated alongside irrigation ditches. A detailed description of such a garden belonging to Merodach-baladan has been preserved. It included date palms and trees bearing apricots, plums, peaches, figs, and pomegranates. The sesame plant was cultivated for oil. Gourds and melons are also mentioned. Since this was a royal garden we must not take it as typical, but it does indicate the possibilities of life during exilic times. Among the other products of Merodach-baladan's garden we read of garlic, onion, leeks, mint, saffron, coriander, rue, thyme, pistacio, lettuce, fennel, lentils, beets, and kohl-rabi. The royal table did not lack variety!

Such houses with gardens were usually located at the outskirts of the towns. Within the towns, houses tended to be huddled together toward the center. Houses were successively rebuilt on the roughly leveled debris of earlier ones. The household rubbish would be thrown into the streets to be eaten by dogs and scavenger animals. What was not devoured would be left to burn dry by the sun and be trodden under foot.

The early houses of Babylon had been made of intertwined branches which were covered with thatch and cemented with mud which, when hardened, held the framework together. In very early times these buildings were round and had a central post like a tent. Later such structures were used as stables or sheepfolds.

Babylonian homes of the exilic period were built with bricks of clay mixed with finely chopped straw. The bricks were formed in molds and dried in the sun. Fired bricks were only used for special buildings because of the high expense of fuel. Sun-dried bricks were used when they were three-quarters dry. These were bonded together with mortar made of diluted clay. Houses were built around a central courtyard which provided light for the rooms which led off from it. One room was provided with a narrow door which led to the street.

Floors were normally made of beaten earth. The well-to-do might use flagstone or baked brick, sloped slightly to the center so the rain water and waste could be drained away. Drainage was provided by terra-cotta conduits which carried the water into underground cesspools. We even find toilets made of flagstones with a hole in the center.

Along the courtyard wall we frequently find the kitchen range. A hole was cut in the wall to allow the smoke to leave the room, or it found its way out through the door. Water was kept in earthen jars half sunk in the courtyard. Jars containing grain would hang from the walls out of reach of the rats and mice. An ingenious method of air vents was devised to keep out the rodents. Channels were cut through the walls, but they were then blocked with terra-cotta tiles pierced with holes which let the air in but kept out the rats and mice.

In a middle class home we would find mats, rugs, or mattresses used as beds. The more wealthy people had high beds with one end built up to form a bolster. The poorer folk sat on stools of palm wood and ate from raised trays which served as tables. The wealthy enjoyed the luxury of chairs, with deeply curved reed backs. They ate from high tables. On such tables there were numerous bowls and dippers made of terra-cotta. Early lamps were in the form of a shallow saucer with a pointed spout for the wick. By exilic times, lamps in the shape of a pointed shoe were in use, with wicks placed in a hole at the point. Unrefined crude oil was used in these lamps.

The roof of a Babylonian house was made of planks of palm wood arranged so as to span its rooms. The wood was then covered with reeds and palm leaves, on top of which a layer of earth was leveled and packed tight by a stone roller. From time to time, particularly after storms, the roof needed repair. The roller was again used and the roof was firm until the next storm.

An outside stairway usually led from the courtyard to the roof which served as a comfortable family room where the cool evening breezes could be enjoyed. In the summer the roof provided a comfortable place for sleeping. Houses of the poorer folk were undecorated except for a whitewash which concealed the drab, clay wall. Those who could afford to do so frequently painted their rooms halfway from the floor to the ceiling. This would often be in a black color derived from diluted bitumen. Above this area they would paint a decorative band in some other color. Door frames were often red, a color thought to keep away demons and guard against the evil influences which might attack a house.

Along the rivers and canals of ancient Babylonia the Israelites would have seen numerous boats conveying both people and merchandise. Small boats were frequently propelled by poles in the calm water. Sails were sometimes made of matting, and an oar at the stern would serve as a rudder. These boats could be hired by those who had temporary need of them.

Some boats still seen on the Tigris and Euphrates rivers are similar in design to those used since Sumerian times. A basket-type boat known as the coracle is made of plaited rushes. Its flat bottom is covered with skins and caulked. One or two men propel the coracle with oars.

Cargo was frequently shipped on a *kelek,* the name given to a raft made of strong reeds or wood. The under surface of the *kelek* was given support by inflated goatskins which were attached to add buoyancy and enable the raft to carry a heavy load.

Individuals frequently crossed the rivers of Babylon on inflated goatskins which served as a kind of life preserver. The

head and the hoofs of the animal were cut off and the skin inflated. This was then placed beneath the chest of the man who
would then use it to cross a stream. Whole armies crossed rivers
on these inflated goatskins. Waterways were also crossed on floats
made of reeds. A quantity of reeds would be bound at each end
and flattened in the center to form such a float. The rivers and
canals had a good supply of fish which formed an important part
of the diet of the people of Babylon. Fish were usually caught on
the line, but nets were also used.

While in Babylon, the Jews adopted a calendar which, with
refinements dating from the fourth century A.D., is still the basis
for the reckoning of the Jewish year. The Babylonians had a
year of twelve lunar months, each consisting of thirty days. They
early learned that this differed considerably from the solar year
of approximately 365¼ days. To make the lunar and solar years
coincide it was necessary to add an intercalary month (Second
Adar) every sixth year. The twelve months, with Babylonian and
Jewish names are:

Hebrew Name	Babylonian Name	Corresponding Months
Nisan	Nisannu	March-April
Iyyar	Ayaru	April-May
Sivan	Simanu	May-June
Tammuz	Du'uzu	June-July
Av	Abu	July-August
Elul	Ululu	August-September
Tishri	Tashretu	September-October
Marsheshvan	Arakshamna	October-November
Kislev	Kislimu	November-December
Tevet	Tabetu	December-January
Shevat	Shabatu	January-February
Adar	Addaru	February-March

The Babylonians reckoned their days from sunset to sunset,
as did the Hebrews (cf. Gen. 1:5). The names of Hebrew months
based upon the Babylonian calendar only appear in post-exilic
writings: Nisan in Nehemiah 2:1; Esther 3:7; and Adar in Ezra
6:15. Years were designated according to the year of the mon-
arch's rule both in Neo-Babylonian and in Persian times. This
was normal Biblical usage both before and after the Exile (cf.
II Kings 22:3; Jer. 25:1; Ezra 1:1; 6:15).

During the Exile a change took place in the speech habits of
the Jews. Their language in pre-exilic days was Hebrew. At the
time of Sennacherib's siege of Jerusalem, Aramaic was the language of diplomatic communication between Assyria and the
provinces of western Asia. The Rab-shakeh addressed his challenge to the people of Jerusalem in the Hebrew language, much
to the distress of Hezekiah's officials who informed him that they

could speak the official Aramaic. The Rab-shakeh, however, wanted the populace to understand his message, so he spoke in the vernacular of the time (II Kings 18:17-37).

Aramaic became the language of diplomacy in the Persian Empire. It is possible that the Aramaic letters to and from Artaxerxes and Darius in the Book of Ezra (Ezra 4:11-22; 5:7-17; 6:6-12; 7:11-26) are actually copies of original texts kept in the Persian archives.

During the Exile, the Jews doubtless learned Aramaic as a means of communication with their non-Jewish neighbors. When they returned to Jerusalem they carried their newly learned language with them. It remained the vernacular language of Syria and Palestine until the Arab conquest of the seventh century A.D. It was the daily language of Palestine during New Testament times.

Hebrew, however, continued to be a living language after the return. The writings of Haggai, Zechariah, and Malachi were written in Hebrew, as were the writings of the Qumran community. Most of the people, however, spoke only Aramaic. When Ezra read the Law to the men of Jerusalem it was necessary to give an interpretation, probably in the Aramaic tongue (Neh. 8:8). Although most of the Old Testament was written in Hebrew, Aramaic was the language used in Daniel 2:4b-7:28 and Ezra 4:8 — 6:18; 7:12-26.

Life during the exile was highly diversified. Although most Jews doubtless practiced agriculture as a means of livelihood, some ultimately entered business. During the Persian period the Murashu family of Nippur operated an important mercantile house.[1] Other Jews became trusted men in government. The Zoroastrian Persians looked with favor on the monotheistic Jews whose lives were lived on a plane much higher than that of most Persian subjects.

---

1. See p. 127.

9

NEBUCHADNEZZAR'S BABYLON

A clay tablet which dates back to Persian times contains a map of the world. Various towns are marked, along with the canals and waterways which made them possible. Around the whole span of the earth's surface is an ocean which has the appearance of a tire on a wheel. Beyond are yet other regions, indicated by triangles which touch the outer rim of the ocean. The geographical center of this universe, however, was the city of Babylon.

Babylon was an ancient city. We are told that Nimrod began his ancient empire there (Gen. 10:10). About 1830 B.C. a dynasty of kings from Babylon began to annex surrounding city-states and the First Dynasty of Babylon began its quest for power. The famed Hammurabi codified Babylonian law (*ca.* 1700 B.C.) and ruled all of southern Mesopotamia, extending his conquests as far as Mari on the middle Euphrates.

The glory of Babylon declined and southern Mesopotamia was ruled for centuries by governors appointed by the Assyrians who ruled from Asshur and Nineveh. When, under Nabopolassar, the Babylonians rebelled against Assyria and, in 612 B.C., helped destroy Nineveh, the center of empire, if not the center of the universe, could be identified with the ancient Babylon.

Our knowledge of ancient Babylon comes from a variety of sources. It is described in the Bible as the capital city of the nation which took Judah into captivity. Daniel and his companions were trained as courtiers in the schools of Babylon. The Greek historian Herodotus, who wrote a century and a half after Nebuchadnezzar, described the city as a vast square, 480 stades (55¼ miles) in circumference, surrounded by a huge moat of running water, beyond which were ramparts two hundred cubits high and fifty cubits broad! Herodotus tells us that the streets were arranged at right angles, a fact later verified by Koldewey, the excavator of Babylon. The Euphrates was walled on both sides as it made its course through the city, a series of gates providing the inhabitants of Babylon access to the river.[1] Diodorus Siculus and other Greeks spoke in admiration of Babylon, unquestionably the largest and most magnificent city of the ancient world.

The Book of Daniel records the boast of Nebuchadnezzar, "Is not this great Babylon that I have built?" (Dan. 4:30). The words are not without meaning. In addition to the walls which surrounded Babylon, Nebuchadnezzar was personally responsible for much that was within the city. He laid out and paved with bricks the great Procession Way which led to the temple of Marduk. The palace of his father Nabopolassar was completely rebuilt. Beams of cedar were imported from distant Lebanon for the project.

Nabopolassar had already begun the rebuilding of Babylon, but it was left to Nebuchadnezzar to pursue the work in earnest. Before the death of Nabopolassar about two-thirds of the work he had planned for the protection of Babylon had been completed. The inner wall of the city, known as Imgur-Bel, was finished. He also had built an outer wall, the Nimitti-Bel, and reconstructed the city gates with cedar wood covered with strips of bronze. Symbolic guardians of the city were the half-human, half-animal bronze colossi which stood at the threshold.

Nebuchadnezzar took up where his father left off. A third massive wall was built on the east side of the city at a distance of four thousand cubits from the outer wall. Before this was a moat, walled around with bricks. Similar defenses were built on the west, but they were not as strong because the desert formed a natural barrier.

To the north, the direction from which trouble might be expected, Nebuchadnezzar pursued a different plan. Between the two walls, and between the river and the Ishtar Gate he constructed an artificial platform of brick laid in bitumen. Upon this elevated platform he built a citadel which was connected with his royal palace. In this way he made the north wall so solid that it could be neither broken down nor breached. The citadel could be used as a watch-tower and, if need be, destructive missiles could be shot or thrown from it upon any enemy who might have reached the outside of the walls. Apart from the possibility of treachery within, Babylon appeared impregnable.

---

1. Herodotus, *Histories*, I, 178-187.

Ruins of Ancient Babylon. Covered for centuries by soil and debris, the spade of the archaeologist now makes it possible for us to trace the buildings and thoroughfares which were the pride of Nebuchadnezzar. Courtesy, Oriental Institute

Babylon at the Time of the Exile. A careful study of the ruins of Babylon formed the basis for this reconstruction of the city as it was in Nebuchadnezzar's time. The painting is by Maurice Barden, based on E. Unger's reconstruction.
Courtesy, Oriental Institute

The Neo-Babylonian period is well documented, and Nebuchadnezzar has left us accounts of his building operation. In
describing his work on the walls he declares:

> Nebuchadrezzar, king of Babylon, the restorer of Esagila and Ezida, son
> of Nabopolassar am I. As a protection to Esagila, that no powerful enemy
> and destroyer might take Babylon, that the line of battle might not ap-
> proach Imgur-Bel, the wall of Babylon, that which no former king had
> done, I did; at the enclosure of Babylon I made an enclosure of a strong
> wall on the east side. I dug a moat, I reached the level of the water. I
> then saw that the wall which my father had prepared was too small in
> its construction. I built with bitumen and brick a mighty wall which, like
> a mountain, could not be moved, and connected it with the wall of my
> father; I laid its foundations on the breast of the underworld; its top I
> raised up like a mountain. Along this wall to strengthen it I constructed
> a third, and as the base of a protecting wall I laid a foundation of bricks,
> and built it on the breast of the under-world, and laid its foundation. The
> fortifications of Esagila and Babylon I strengthened, and established the
> name of my reign forever.[2]

Archaeology has provided us with the tools to evaluate the
boasts of Nebuchadnezzar and the reports of Herodotus. In 1898
Robert Koldewey began the excavation of Babylon under the
auspices of the *Deutsche Orientgesellschaft.* Work continued for
more than eighteen years. Full reports of Koldewey's work appeared in his book, *Das wieder erstehende Babylon,* which contained photographs and plans of the city and its principal structures. The foreword to the first edition was dated, "Babylon, May
16, 1912." A fourth edition appeared in 1925.

Koldewey came upon the walls of Babylon during the early
days of his dig. It took considerable time to excavate them, but
the results were indeed impressive. Around the ruins of the city
was a brick wall 22-1/3 feet thick. Outside this wall was a space
38-1/3 feet wide, then another brick wall, 25 feet thick. If the
outer wall were breached the invader would find himself trapped
between two walls. Lining the inner side of the citadel moat was
still another wall, 12 feet thick. In times of danger the moat
could be flooded.

The walls were surmounted every 160 feet by watchtowers.
Koldewey suggests that there were 360 such towers on the inner
wall (an estimate based upon the pattern of the ruins). Excavations indicate that the towers were 27 feet wide, and they probably were 90 feet high (much less than the 300 feet mentioned
by Herodotus). Ancient historians tell us that two chariots could
be driven abreast on the road which ran on top of the wall and

---

2. Translation by G. A. Barton, *Archaeology and the Bible,* pp. 478-479,
from *Zeitschrift fur Assyriologie,* I, 337 f.

completely surrounded the city. The walls were constantly pa-trolled by guards.

There were numerous gates in the walls, although Herodotus' reference to one hundred gates must be dismissed as hyperbole. The most famous entrance into the city was the Ishtar gate which led from the north of the city into the Procession Way. The gate was fifteen feet wide and its vaulted passageway was thirty-five feet above the street level. The bricks were so molded that they form bas-relief figures of bulls and dragons. Their surfaces were overlaid with thickly colored enamels. Nebuchadnezzar used properly fired bricks, and they have remained through the ages. The sun baked bricks used by his predecessors have disintegrated long ago.

The Procession Way was primarily used for the great annual occasion when king and people went to the temple of Marduk at the New Year's Festival. During the forty-three years of his reign, Nebuchadnezzar continued to beautify the Procession Way. He wrote:

> Aibur-shabu, the street of Babylon, I filled with a high fill for the pro-cession of the great lord Marduk, and with Turminabanda stones and Shadu stones I made this Aibur-shabu fill for the procession of his godli-ness, and linked it with those parts which my father had built, and made the way a shining one.[3]

The pavement of the Procession Way was built over a base of bricks covered with bitumen. It consisted of blocks of limestone with sides more than a yard wide, pointed with asphalt. Inscribed on the underside of each of the slabs were the words:

> Nebuchadnezzar, King of Babylon, son of Nabopolassar, King of Baby-lon, am I. Of the streets of Babylon for the procession of the great lord Marduk, with slabs of limestone, I built the causeway. Oh, Marduk my lord, grant eternal life.[4]

Along the walls of the Procession Way was a series of 120 lions in enameled relief. They were spaced at 64 foot intervals and gave a sense of awe to the street. The lions had hides of white or yellow, with manes of yellow or red. They were posed against a background of light or dark blue. The Procession Way was 73½ feet wide.

At the annual New Year's Festival, statues of the principal deities were assembled from all the provinces of the kingdom and solemnly carried through the Ishtar Gate out to the north-ern outskirts of the city. There they were transferred to boats and taken to the Garden Temple up the river. This was followed

---

3. Hugo Winckler, *Keilinschrift. Bibl.*, III, part 2, pp. 60-61.
4. From R. Campbell Thompson, "The New Babylonian Empire," in *The Cambridge Ancient History*, III, p. 217.

by the consummation of the sacred marriage of the principal god and goddess, which was presumed to guarantee the fertility and prosperity of the whole land. On the eleventh day of the month Nisan the procession joyously returned through the Ishtar Gate from the north. Marduk led the procession in his chariot-boat. Behind the chief god of Babylon rode the king in his chariot. Behind the king were carriage-boats containing the images of the other gods worshiped in Babylon.

Along the Procession Way was the famous staged-tower or zig-gurat of Babylon known as E-temen-anki — "The House of the Foundation of Heaven and Earth" — which rose 300 feet into the air and could be seen from a distance by travelers approaching the city. Fifty-eight million bricks are said to have been used in its construction. Like Babylon itself, the ziggurat goes back to remote antiquity. On its top was a Temple to Marduk, the god of Babylon. Enemies of the state — such as Tukulti-Ninurta, Sargon, Sennacherib, and Ashurbanipal — devastated the city and destroyed the Marduk shrine. The tower was rebuilt by the Neo-Babylonian rulers Nabopolassar and Nebuchadnezzar. In a sense it pictured both the glories of Marduk, and of Marduk's city, Babylon. Nabopolassar declared:

> The lord Marduk commanded me concerning E-temen-anki, the staged tower of Babylon, which before my time had become dilapidated and ruinous, that I should make its foundations secure in the bosom of the nether world, and make its summit like the heavens.[5]

The ziggurat consisted of seven terraces, on the top of which was a temple made of bricks enameled bright blue to represent the heavens. The temple was approached by a triple staircase, at the middle of which there was a place where the visitor might rest. Within the temple was a couch and a golden table. This was regarded as the abode of Marduk. No one except a priestess, who served as the consort of the god, was to enter this shrine. The prosperity of the land was thought to depend upon this sacred marriage ritual.

Across the street from the ziggurat was the temple area known as E-sag-ila ("The house which lifts up the head"). Herodotus visited the E-sag-ila and was much impressed by its golden figure of "Zeus" (Babylonian Bel-Marduk) seated in the shrine beside a golden table. According to the statistics which Herodotus gives (which may be exaggerated) the gold of these objects weighed about 800 talents, or 4800 pounds with a current value of $24,000,000. "Zeus" appeared as a half-animal, half-human creature.

---

5. André Parrot, *The Tower of Babel,* p. 18.

Outside the sanctuary were a number of other altars and statues including a standing figure of Marduk, twelve cubits (twenty feet) high, of solid gold. The complex of buildings occupied sixty acres, bounded on the west by the Euphrates and on the east by the Procession Way. Towering 470 feet above the ground was the shrine known as the E-kur ("Temple mountain") built on a terrace of asphalted bricks like the nearby ziggurat.

The total number of shrines in ancient Babylon, as recorded in contemporary inscriptions, appears incredible. We read that,

> There are altogether in Babylon fifty-three temples of the great gods, fifty-five shrines dedicated to Marduk, three hundred shrines belonging to earth divinities, six hundred shrines for celestial divinities, one hundred and eighty altars to the goddess Ishtar, one hundred and eighty to the gods Nergal and Adad, and twelve other altars to various deities.[6]

North of the ziggurat was a mound called Kasr on which Nebuchadnezzar built the most imposing of his palaces. The palace walls were of finely made yellow brick, and floors were of white and mottled sandstone. The palace was adorned with reliefs in blue glaze. Its gates were guarded by gigantic basalt lions.

Near the palace were the famed Hanging Gardens, considered to be one of the Seven Wonders of the Ancient World. Nebuchadnezzar built the gardens for his wife who missed the hills of her Median homeland. The gardens appear to have been terraced and set on a small hill beside the palace, flanked by the Procession Way and the Ishtar Gate.

Josephus quotes from Berossus, *History of Chaldea,* an account of the building of Nebuchadnezzar's palace and the hanging gardens,

> In this palace he erected retaining walls of stone to which he gave an appearance very like that of mountains and, by planting on them trees of all kinds, he achieved this effect and built the so-called hanging garden because his wife, who had been brought up in the region of Media, had a desire for her native environment.[7]

The gardens were irrigated by means of an endless chain of buckets which raised water to the highest point of the terrace. The gardens were impressive when viewed from a distance from the city. The visitor to Babylon could see the tops of the trees towering above the city walls.

Nebuchadnezzar's Babylon was an excellent example of early city planning. The city was divided into a number of rectangles by wide roads which were named after the gods of the Babylonian pantheon. On the left bank of the Euphrates we find the streets of Marduk and Zababa intersecting at right angles with

---

6. Quoted in M. Rutten, *Babylone*, p. 47.
7. Josephus, *Antiquities*, X, 226.

the streets of Sin and Enlil. On the right bank we find an inter-
section of the streets of Adad and Shamash. Except for the
famed Procession Way, Babylon's streets were not paved.

A bridge connecting the eastern or New City with the western
city of Babylon had stone piers and a timber foot path which
could be withdrawn in times of emergency. Permanent bridges
were rare in the ancient East, and the one across the Euphrates
was a source of wonder to travelers.

The business life of the city centered in the wharves which
flanked the Euphrates. Business offices were located along the
river bank. The market sector of ancient Babylon has not been
identified, but it was probably located in the *Merkes* quarter.

The houses of the city were frequently three or four stories
high, being built according to a pattern which has been familiar
in the East from ancient times to the present. Each home would
be built around a central courtyard. There would be no windows
facing the street, but all light would come through the courtyard. Access to the rooms of the second story was by a wooden
balcony which extended around the entire inner courtyard. A
narrow door in one of the first floor rooms opened into the street.

Ancient Babylon required a system of canals if the best use
was to be made of the waters of the Tigris and the Euphrates.
Hammurabi, the famed king of the Old Babylonian Empire had
been a canal builder, and his successors needed to be careful to
insure proper irrigation of the fields. When Nebuchadnezzar
came to the throne of Babylon, its eastern canal had so deteriorated that there were places where its channel could not be
traced. Nebuchadnezzar had it redug, and then walled up from
the bottom. Because the canal passed through Babylon, it was
necessary to build a bridge across it.

Although most of his energy was spent on Babylon itself,
Nebuchadnezzar did not completely neglect the other cities of
Mesopotamia. He rebuilt the walls of Borsippa and restored the
temples of the city to a good state of repair.

Nebuchadnezzar was an able and an energetic sovereign. He
was in all respects the most able as well as the most ambitious
ruler of his day. In him the Neo-Babylonian Empire reached its
zenith. Great as were his accomplishments both on the field of
battle and in building the cities of his kingdom, Nebuchadnezzar
left an empire that had no political stability. His own personality
held it together, and when that was gone it was not long before
his dynasty came to an end.

10

THE WISDOM OF THE BABYLONIANS

Daniel was expected to become proficient in the "letters and language of the Chaldeans" (Dan. 1:4). He was enrolled in a school and given the ancient equivalent of a liberal education. The Babylonia of Daniel's day preserved its records on clay or stone. A scribe would use a stylus to cut cuneiform (i.e., "wedge-shaped") characters on a soft piece of clay. When baked in the sun, this would become a permanent record.

The cuneiform method of writing was adopted by the Semitic peoples of the Fertile Crescent as a result of contacts with the Sumerians who first used it as a means of communication shortly before 3000 B.C. The Sumerians, like the Egyptians, began with a system of picture writing. It was the nature of the writing material of Sumer that produced cuneiform. The stylus used for writing on clay tablets could be used most efficiently in forming wedges on the soft clay. Pictures early became conventionalized into groups of wedges, and the pictorial character of the language was lost.

In the earliest stage of the language, signs stood for the objects which they represented. In time, however, the signs came to represent syllables with no necessary relationship to their origin. With this development, any word in the language could be written. If we were to adopt such a system, a conventionalized picture of a cat would represent our noun "cat." As a syllable, the symbol could represent the first part of the word catalogue, or catacomb, or any word beginning with "cat." If we worshiped the cat, its symbol, prefixed by a sign representing deity, could also represent the cat-god. If our culture conceived of the cat as a sly creature, we might even use the cat symbol to represent the verb "to be sly." In such a usage the syllable "cat-" would not have to appear in the verb. The reader would know that the verb "to be sly" was meant in a given context.

The Sumerian writing system was indeed cumbersome, but it did make possible written communication in all its forms — religious epics, historical annals, law codes, personal letters, contracts, receipts, and all that makes possible civilization as we know it. The alphabet, a much more efficient system of written communication, did not completely replace cuneiform until shortly before the time of Christ. Cuneiform writing was used for the thousands of ancient records which archaeologists use in reconstructing the history of the ancient Near East. The fact that they were written on clay renders them almost indestructible as compared with papyrus and leather which quickly deteriorate in moist climates.

Our finest collection of cuneiform literature comes from the library of Ashurbanipal, the Assyrian ruler known as Osnapper in the Old Testament (Ezra 4:10). Ashurbanipal was characterized both by ruthlessness and culture. A relief shows him in the royal garden enjoying a banquet with Ashur-sharrat, his wife. The scene is almost idyllic until we note, hanging from a coniferous tree, the head of an Elamite chieftain whom he had conquered.

On the other hand, Ashurbanipal boasts of his education and culture. He writes:

> I, Ashurbanipal, learned the wisdom of Nabu, the entire art of writing on clay tablets . . . . I learned to shoot the bow, to ride, to drive and to seize the reins.
> I received the revelation of the wise Adapa, the hidden treasure of the art of writing . . . . I considered the heavens with the learned masters . . . . I read the beautiful clay tablets from Sumer and the obscure Akkadian writing which is hard to master. I had my joy in the reading of inscriptions on stone from the time before the flood . . . . The following were my daily activities: I mounted my horse, I rode joyfully . . . I held the bow . . . I go around . . . . At the same time I learned royal decorum and walked in kingly ways.[1]

Ashurbanipal's library was discovered in 1853 by Hormuzd Rassam, the brother of the British vice-consul at Mosul, who was continuing the work of Austin Henry Layard. We gain some idea of the literary resources of the seventh century before Christ when we realize that the library contained over 22,000 clay tablets containing religious, literary, and scientific works. Among these were the Babylonian creation and flood epics.

Tablets in Ashurbanipal's collection came from a variety of sources. Many were copied from originals by his own scribes. He dispatched officials to the cities of his Empire with orders to gather all texts of importance. One of his extant directives ends

---

1. Quoted in Jack Finegan, *Light from the Ancient Past,* pp. 216-217.

with the words, "If you hear of any tablet or ritualistic text that is suitable for the palace, seek it out, secure it, and send it here."

A writing system as complex as cuneiform required a class of professional scribes to read and write the numerous documents required by an advanced culture. Scribal schools were the centers of learning in the ancient Near East. A number of cuneiform "textbooks" were discovered at the site of ancient Shuruppak, the home town of the Sumerian Noah, in 1902-03. A scribal school is known to have been conducted at Shuruppak around 2500 B.C. Archaeologists have discovered hundreds of practice tablets from a later period. We can read on them the actual exercises prepared by pupils as a part of their school work.

Since the scribe represented a learned profession, it might be expected that recruits would come from the upper level of society. A German cuneiformist, Nikolaus Schneider, studied thousands of published economic and administrative documents from about 2000 B.C. and found the names of about five hundred individuals who listed themselves as scribes. Many of them listed the name and occupation of their fathers. These include temple administrators, priests, military officers, ambassadors, sea captains, accountants, high tax officials, other scribes, and the like. All appear to have been wealthy citizens of urban communities.[2]

Although a youth might be able to enter a scribal school because of the wealth or influence of his father, nevertheless he would have to prove himself by careful attention to his studies. The scribe was honored as a member of a learned profession, but he gained competence only through years of hard work.

I. Literature

Among the great religious writings of the time when Daniel would have gone to school in Babylon was the *Enuma Elish,* the Babylonian account of creation. The Babylonians believed that the world originated in Chaos — a waste of waters with Apsu (sweet water) and Tiamat (salt water) constituting the primordial elements. From these deities other gods were formed. The theogony was patterned after human life, with the gods arranged according to sex and generation. For some reason the great gods Anu, Enlil, and Ea aroused the wrath of Apsu and Tiamat, and the older gods determined to rid themselves of their offspring.

2. See Samuel N. Kramer, *From the Tablets of Sumer,* p. 5.

Ea, however, was able to destroy Apsu, a fact which enraged
Tiamat, who gave birth to eleven horrible monsters, their leader
being named Kingu. She expected them to avenge the death of
Apsu and subdue the rebellious gods. In the meantime, the kindly Ea gave birth to a son, Marduk, who was destined to save the
gods from Tiamat's murderous plan.

Terrorized by Tiamat and her monsters, the gods looked for
some way to destroy her. Marduk accepted the suggestion that
he be their champion on condition that he be given absolute
authority over all the gods, and that his decisions be accepted as
final. The gods, helpless against the wrath of Tiamat, agreed to
his conditions.

After suitable preparation, Marduk was ready for his encounter with Tiamat. As she prepared to devour him, Marduk cast
one of the four winds of heaven into her open mouth, and thrust
his sword into her distended body. In this way Tiamat was killed
and her body cut in two. From one half of her corpse Marduk
made the sky, and with the other half he formed the earth. Subsequently he created man, and Kingu — who had been taken captive — provided the necessary blood.

Although at first glance fantastic, the *Enuma Elish* was de-
signed to teach some important lessons. One of them was political. Marduk was the god of Babylon, and the story tells how his
place of supremacy was recognized by all the other gods. If the
god of Babylon is the greatest of gods, then Babylon itself must
be the greatest of cities and have a divine right to rule all others.
There are other forms of the creation story, but the one promul-
gated in Babylon sought to justify the supremacy of Babylon.
This is not to suggest that the story was maliciously invented to
serve utilitarian ends. On the contrary, when Babylon became a
world power, her success was considered an evidence of the
power of her god. Since Babylon's armies had destroyed other nations, her god must have been supreme!

The fact that human blood finds its origin in the evil Kingu
is not an accident, either. Although not possessing the moral con-
sciousness of the Hebrew prophets, nevertheless the Babylonians
knew that man tended to be perverse in his ways. Why is man
such a rebellious fellow? The *Enuma Elish* gives the answer —
Man has the blood of Kingu.

The famous Gilgamesh Epic probably dates back to the third
millennium before Christ. Fragments of it have been discovered
in the Hittite and Hurrian languages, and it probably was translated into many others as well. The theme of the Gilgamesh Epic

is man, with his struggles and hopes. This may be the reason for
its popularity.

Gilgamesh, the tyrant of Erech, was part human and part divine. He acted in such a highhanded way that the people cried
to their gods for deliverance. The gods thereupon formed Enkidu, who was a bull from the waist down and human from the
waist up. Enkidu was destined to oppose and vanquish Gilgamesh.

We first meet Enkidu in the fields where he was a friend of
the wild animals. He released them from traps and helped them
to thwart hunters. One day, however, a hunter saw Enkidu and
told his father about this unusual being. The father sent his son
to find a girl who would bring about a change in Enkidu's character. The girl, Shamhat, was brought to Enkidu. She had carnal
relations with him, whereupon he became a changed creature.
He accompanied her to Erech, ate bread instead of grass, drank
from vessels, anointed himself with oil, and put on clothes. Enkidu had been introduced to human culture, and would never
again be at home in the world of the wild animals.

Eventually Enkidu and Gilgamesh met. Instead of fighting one
another they decided to join forces to slay dragons and help the
cause of righteousness to triumph. After his victory over the drag-
on Humbaba in the Cedar Forest, the goddess Ishtar proposed
marriage to Gilgamesh. The ruler of Erech spurned the goddess, however. He reminded her of her long and shameful record.
She had loved a horse, then beat him. A shepherd whom she loved
was later turned into a wolf. Gilgamesh could not permit himself
to become entangled with such a woman! She, however, was a
goddess, and determined to punish him for his impertinence.
Ishtar asked the Bull of Heaven (a human-headed bull) to kill
Gilgamesh, but Gilgamesh and Enkidu managed to kill the Bull
of Heaven, instead. Enkidu cut off a leg from the Bull of Heaven
and threw it at Ishtar. She could not let this insult go unpun-
ished, so she plotted his death.

The death of Enkidu brought Gilgamesh face to face with
life's starkest reality. Gilgamesh, mourning his friend, determined to find immortality for himself. A man named Utnapishtim was the one mortal who had achieved immortality, and Gilgamesh set out to find him in order that he might learn his
secret. Along the way Gilgamesh met a barmaid who tried to
dissuade him from his quest, urging him to enjoy the present
life and forget about the uncertain future. Gilgamesh continued
his quest, however, until he found Utnapishtim.

The story which Utnapishtim told to Gilgamesh is familiar to Bible students, because it contains the Akkadian parallel to the Biblical flood story. In the Babylonian version, the gods determined to rid themselves of mankind by means of a flood. The kindly Ea warned Utnapishtim of the impending flood and urged him to build an ark in which he might save the lives of his family and of representative members of the animal creation. Utnapishtim obeyed the word of Ea, built the ark, and not only saved his life but procured immortality for himself as well.

Gilgamesh, however, did not achieve immortality. Utnapishtim challenged him to remain awake for a week, but he was unable to do so. As a substitute for immortality Utnapishtim gave Gilgamesh a magic plant which had the power to rejuvenate him. The possession of this plant guaranteed that its owner would become young again — an early form of the "fountain of youth" motif. Tragedy struck, however, for when Gilgamesh paused for a drink of water, the plant slipped from him and was swallowed by a snake. As a result, the serpent can shed its old skin and become rejuvenated, but man must face the certainty of old age and death! Gilgamesh continued his journey to Erech. If he had not gained immortality, he at least could admire his earthly abode.

The gods of the Gilgamesh Epic possess thoroughly human characteristics. They not only strive with one another, but they are so famished at the end of the flood that, as Utnapishtim prepares sacrifices for them, "The gods smelt the sweet savour: like flies they gathered together over him that sacrificed."[3]

The Gilgamesh Epic probably contains the memory of real floods which covered much of the Tigris-Euphrates area. Such floods took place at the end of the last ice age (*ca.* 8000 B.C.) and may be reflected in both the Biblical and the Babylonian accounts.

2. Mathematics

The Babylonians inherited the sexagesimal system from the ancient Sumerians. This system of numbering by sixties is still in use. We reckon sixty seconds to the minute, and sixty minutes to the hour. The system is also used in the division of the circle into three hundred and sixty degrees.

---

3. *The Gilgamesh Epic,* XI, lines 160-161.

The cuneiform syllabary was adapted to the writing of mathematical texts. An upright stroke would mean either "one" or "sixty" depending on its position and context. An angular stroke stood for the number ten. The system was such that any number could be written, although the concept of zero, and its usefulness as a mathematical symbol were not known.

Mathematical problems which have been preserved for us on cuneiform tablets show that by 2000 B.C. the Babylonians could measure the area of rectangles and of right and isoceles triangles. Subsequently we know that they could calculate the exact volume of a pyramid and of a truncated cone. The mathematical value of pi was defined as three, an approximation of our more accurate 3.1416.

An amazing knowledge of algebra is also shown in the Babylonian literature. From the Old Babylonian period we have tablets of squares, square roots, cubes, and cube roots. We even find tables of the sums of squares and cubes needed for the numerical solution of special types of cubic equations. Babylonian mathematical texts prove that the Pythagorean theorem was known more than a thousand years before Pythagoras.[4]

3. Astronomy

Closely related to Babylonian mathematics, and using it as an important tool, was the science of astronomy. By 800 B.C. Babylonian astronomers had attained sufficient accuracy to assign positions to the stars and note their heliacal settings. An attempt was made to determine cause and effect relationships between the motions of the heavenly bodies and purely human events. If an eclipse was once followed by a war with Elam, a second eclipse might be considered the portent of another such war. Astronomers of this period reported regularly to the court concerning their observations. In taunting the proud Babylonians, Isaiah said, "You are wearied with your many counsels; let them stand forth and save you, those who divide the heavens, who gaze at the stars, who at the new moons predict what shall befall you" (Isa. 47:13).

During this period no distinction was made between astronomical and meteorological phenomena. Clouds were reported in the same way as eclipses. Through observation, however, astronomers noted that solar eclipses could take place only at the end of the month, and lunar eclipses only at the middle.

---

4. O. Neugebauer, *The Exact Sciences in Antiquity*, p. 36.

A cuneiform tablet from about 700 B.C. classifies the fixed stars. They were arranged on three "roads," the middle of which was an equatorial belt of 30° width. The Road of Enlil contained thirty-three stars, that of Anu, twenty-three, and that of Ea only fifteen. A companion tablet discusses the planets, the moon, the seasons, the lengths of the shadow, and related problems. A distinction is made between planets, termed "wild goats" because they wandered in the heavens, and fixed stars, or "tame goats" because they did not roam! The concepts discussed in these tablets are elementary indeed, but they are significant in that they describe astronomical phenomena with no reference to mythological concepts.

By 500 B.C. we find, as the reference system for solar and planetary motion, a zodiac of twelve sections, each thirty degrees in length. The main sequences of planetary and lunar phenomena had been observed. Arithmetical progressions were in use to describe periodically variable quantities. Lengths of daylight and darkness at a given time could be predicted.

The planets were named for the gods of Babylon and, in their Graeco-Roman form, we still so designate them. Ishtar, the Babylonian goddess of love became Venus in the classical world. Similarly Marduk became Jupiter; Nabu, the announcer, became Mercury; Nergal, God of war, became Mars; and Ninib, patron of agriculture, became Saturn. The days of the week were, in Babylonian thought, ruled by the heavenly bodies, and ultimately each of the seven days was devoted to a specific deity. Thus we have the day of the sun, the moon, Nergal (Mars), Marduk (Jupiter), Ishtar (Venus), and Ninib (Saturn). With little variation this is still the order of our week, with first, second, and last days preserving the Roman form of the names. Since our calendar came through a northern route it reflects Norse mythology in such names as Woden's day (Wednesday) and Thor's day (Thursday). All, however, ultimately go back to the gods of ancient Babylon.

The tribal name Chaldean came to be used as a specialized term for astrologer or magician in the Greek and Roman writers.[5] The pseudo-science of astrology came into its own in Seleucid times, and proved attractive to many throughout the classical world.

---

5. Cf. also Dan. 2:2 ff.

4. Medicine

Babylonian medicine was largely associated with concepts of demons and evil spirits and the means of counteracting their harmful spells. The physician-priest was a man noted for his ability to use potent spells to exorcise evil spirits. In the field of surgery, however, real advances were made among the Babylonians. The attempt to learn the will of the gods by an examination of animal entrails furnished, by way of analogy, some idea of human anatomy. As early as the Code of Hammurabi (*ca.* 1700 B.C.) physicians performed delicate operations on the human eye. A surgeon who opened an abscess in a man's eye and blinded him was punished by having his own fingers removed.

5. The Natural Sciences

Babylonian science was the result of observation, and it consistently served practical purposes. Plants and animals were named, and we possess plant lists with Sumerian and Akkadian names listed in parallel columns. Stones are listed and classified. An ancient legend tells us that the great god Ninurta was confronted by an alliance of his enemies. His friends, who came to his aid, and his foes, who sought to overthrow him, were the various types of stones. After his victory, the stones which helped him were assigned beautiful names and became the precious stones which adorn temples and are fashioned into exquisite jewelry. The hostile, defeated stones were assigned menial tasks — they became paving stones, door sills or pebbles on the road.

Chemistry, likewise, served a practical function. Minerals were refined by burning, and unusual alloys were compounded. A type of glass known as "copper-lead" had as its ingredients 60 parts of ordinary glass, 10 of lead, 15 of copper, $\frac{1}{2}$ of saltpeter and $\frac{1}{2}$ of lime. The purity of gold was a constant source of contention. Burra-buriash of Babylon (14th Century B.C.) complained to Amenhotep IV of Egypt that the twenty minas of gold which had been sent to him became five minas of pure gold after the refining process. Tests made on the gold articles discovered in ancient Sumer and Babylon show a wide variety in the purity of the gold of which they were made.

11

BABYLONIAN RELIGION

The religion which the Jews of the Exile found in Babylon had roots which went back over two thousand years. The ancient Sumerian city-states were theoretically under the protection of patron deities. Semitic invaders brought a new set of gods into southern Mesopotamia. Sumerians, Semites, and other settlers were polytheistic and did not object to incorporating new gods and goddesses into their religious scheme. When alliances were made, or conquests achieved, the gods of the city-states were subject to new classifications. The god of a victorious state was considered to be the most powerful deity, for warfare was always waged on two levels. The earthly states were championed by their celestial deities, and the battles in the sky were accounted as real as the battles on earth. Assyrian kings did battle in the might of Asshur, and Babylonian rulers looked to Marduk as their guide and protector.

A modern logician has a difficult time with the religion of ancient Babylon and Assyria. When the Semites entered the Tigris-Euphrates Valley they found the Sumerians worshiping the mother goddess Inanna. This posed no problem, for they simply gave her the Semitic name Ishtar and worshiped her as devoutly as did their Sumerian neighbors. In practice, however, Inanna and Ishtar became two goddesses, for each had her devotees. The deities were classified according to sex and marital status and genealogies, or, more strictly, theogonies were arranged. Since Inanna or Ishtar was the chief goddess we would expect her to be the consort of the chief god. Who was this supreme deity? The people of Asshur, the Assyrians would insist that their god was supreme, and the Babylonians would hail the power of Marduk. Thus Ishtar would be regarded as the wife of different gods, depending upon the city in which the claim was made.

There is, of course, a logic in this very illogical approach to religion. Each people thought its god supreme, and imputed to it those powers and attributes which are usually associated with a great god. To the Assyrians, Asshur was the god responsible for the creation of the universe; to the Babylonians it was Marduk who made all things. In each nation, however, there were numerous other gods who were worshiped. It is the fact of a common religious tradition, coupled with the concept of local patron deities, that produces the illogical pantheons of the eastern Fertile Crescent peoples. Heaven itself was divided into three parts, each assigned to one of the great deities.

During Sumerian times, the chief god was known as An, or Anu, the sky god who was regarded as father of the great gods. In "the heaven of Anu" the other deities gathered in times of festivity or sorrow. It was there that the gods whose earthly shrines were destroyed by the flood found a place of refuge. Anu is represented in the cuneiform characters by a star, symbolic of both the god and his heavenly abode. Cult centers of Anu were located at Der in Akkad and at Uruk in Sumer where the temple known as E-anna ("the house of Anu") was located. An important temple to Anu was located in the *girsu* or holy quarter of Lagash.

Anu was remote from the world of men, and does not seem to have been a popular god. His worship was complemented, however, by that accorded to his daughter Ishtar, who made up for any lack in her father's popularity. Ishtar, the goddess of love, was worshiped along with Anu both at the E-anna of Uruk and the *girsu* of Lagash.

Until the rise of the Marduk cult in Babylon, Anu was reputed to be the supreme deity in the Tigris-Euphrates valley. He possessed the symbols of kingship — scepter and diadem, staff and crown. All subordinate rule was responsible to him.

The second great god, honored alike by Sumerians and Semites, was Enlil or Bel. Bel is another form of the Semitic Baal, a word which means "Lord." Enlil-Bel was the lord, or ruler of earth. His abode was the "Great Mountain" in the heaven of Bel which united heaven and earth. As storm god he was, "Lord of the winds." During Sumerian times his worship was centered at Nippur. Since his domain was the earth, Enlil was closer to the affairs of men than was Anu, his father in the theogony. Enlil is described as "the wise" and "the prudent" but he can, on occasion, bring suffering to the world of men. He defied the wishes of Ea and Ishtar and ordered the onset of the flood which destroyed man and beast. He was also deemed responsible for the destruction of Ur by the Elamites. Through Enlil-Bel, divine power was executed on earth.

Important changes took place in the Enlil cult when Marduk was recognized as supreme god in Babylon. Marduk assumed the name of Bel, and became known as Bel-Marduk. Enlil was then designated, "Bel the ancient." His wife was Belit, the feminine form of the name Bel.

The third of the great Sumerian gods was known as Enki, Semitic Ea. Enki ruled the waters upon which, according to the Babylonian cosmology, the terrestrial world floated. He bore the epithet, "Lord of the watery deep." Some traditions made Enki-Ea the creator of the world. In extravagant language he is called, "King of the abyss, Creator of everything, Lord of all." Like Anu he is even designated as "father of the gods."

Enki-Ea was considered to be both wise and kindly disposed toward mankind. It was he who taught men the art of writing and geometry. From him man learned how to build temples and cities and to cultivate the soil. Magic, medicine, and divination were subject to his control. His kindness toward mankind was exhibited when he warned the Sumero-Babylonian Noah to build an ark as a place of safety in the impending flood. Enki's ancient cult center was at Eridu, at the head of the Persian Gulf.

Anu, Enlil and Ea formed a triad of great gods exercising power over air, earth, and water. There were however, many other gods who demanded the worship and offerings of the people. Some of these had specific functions or were the embodiment of forces of nature. A second generation triad — Sin, the moon-god; Shamash, the sun-god; and Adad, the storm god, largely supplanted the older deities in the popular affection.

The Mesopotamian world ascribed great importance to Sin, the moon god, whose waxing and waning governed the passing of the months. Divination and astrology were largely dependent on the moon, and were closely related to his worship. As with Enki-Ea, wisdom was associated with Sin. In Sumerian times, Sin bore the name Nanna. Both Ur and Haran were devoted to his worship.

Corresponding to Sin, the moon god, we find Shamash, the sun, known to the Sumerians as Utu. Shamash was considered to be the son of Sin. Although westerners might expect the relationship to be reversed, we must remember that the Semite begins his day with sunset. This is the order used in describing the creative days of Genesis: "And it was evening, and it was morning, day one" (Gen. 1:5b). Although welcomed at dawn when the light of day drives away the evil spirits thought to dwell in the darkness, as the day advances Shamash is looked upon as a foe. The heat of the sun parches the land. Activities must cease at midday lest sunstroke and death result from his activities in the hot regions of the Near East.

Shamash, as bringer of light, was also associated in the mind of the ancient Babylonian with justice. He is termed, "the light of things above and things below" and "the supreme judge of heaven and earth who guides aright living creatures." The evil that can lurk under cover of darkness is forced into the open by the appearance of Shamash. As god of justice, it is Shamash who is depicted on the top of the stele containing the law code of King Hammurabi. He was worshiped at shrines in Larsa, in southern Babylonia, and at Sippar, farther north.

Adad, the storm god, was worshiped throughout the Near East. The Aramaeans knew him as Hadad, and his name appears in the Biblical Ben-hadad, the king of Damascus. As a god of fertility, Adad was called, "Lord of abundance, Irrigator of heaven and earth." His home was in the mountain heights from which he could thunder forth with lightning and rain. In the Babylonian flood story it was Adad who let loose the deluge which turned mankind into clay. Since man's life depended, in large measure, on the fertility which Adad could bring, he was a god whose worship was seldom neglected. In Syria and Palestine, Hadad was identified with Baal, who was "rider of the clouds" and through whom fertility was provided for man and beast as well as for the parched fields. Adad's consort was Shala, "lady of the ear of grain."

Fertility and reproduction in the Tigris-Euphrates valley were associated with Ishtar, the popular daughter of Anu. She was also the goddess of war. The Sumerian form of her name, Innana, means "Lady of heaven," and Innana-Ishtar was identified with the planet Venus. She was the great mother goddess of the ancient Near East and, throughout all the changes which the religion of Babylon and Assyria underwent, Ishtar always maintained her independent position. At one time or another she was considered to be the wife of the "great god" of almost every city in Mesopotamia. Her most famous shrine was in Uruk, Biblical Erech.

The priestly theologians of ancient Babylon attempted to breathe order into the confused picture of their historic pantheon which grew more complex with the passing of the years. They classified the status, rank, and function of each of the gods, and developed a hierarchy patterned after human affairs. Gods were grouped into families, and their servants and slaves are indicated. There were four thousand gods in all, many of whom had highly specialized functions. A few, however, will suffice to show the development of the religious life in ancient Baby-lonia.

During the earliest Sumerian period the lord of the *girsu* of Lagash was known as Ninurta, or Enurta. At that time he was a fertility god who was responsible for the annual flooding of the rivers. Early texts symbolize him by the plough, indicating his function of making agriculture possible. In time, however, another side of his character was emphasized. By the late Assyrian period he was symbolized by weapons and he became known as the god of battles.

Semitic Nusku, Sumerian Gibil, was the god of fire. He was invoked by magicians in their tasks of exorcism. They called upon Nusku to burn to death evil spirits and sorcerers. Nusku was also associated with worship, for he made burnt offerings possible.

Nergal had originally been a sun god, but as the destroyer of life (one attribute of the sun god), he went to the nether regions to found a kingdom for himself. There he became the god of pestilence and death. His domain was known as "the land of no return." His wife was Ereshkigal, the sister of Shamash and Ishtar. She had ruled the nether regions before the arrival of Nergal. On his arrival they became husband and wife. The nether regions were also populated by monsters with both human and animal forms.

The scribe of the gods was Nabu (Nebo), the patron of Bor-sippa, who was reputed to have great wisdom. The Table of Fate was in his keeping, and he had power to prolong or shorten life. Nebuchadnezzar's name, meaning, "Nebo has established the boundary," expresses faith in Nebo, identified as a son of Marduk, the great god of Babylon.

During the period of the First Dynasty of Babylon an important revolution took place in the religion of the country. A minor deity named Marduk was chosen as the principal god of the whole of Babylonia. Although the older deities were accorded their accustomed worship, Marduk, a son of Ea, was placed at the head of the pantheon. The *Enuma Elish,* which dates from this time, relates the way in which the gods and goddesses, terrified by the primordial monster, Tiamat (Chaos), appealed for help. The youthful Marduk, on condition that all acknowledge his supremacy, accepted the challenge, slew the monster, and from her corpse created the heaven and the earth. Thus the supremacy of the god of Babylon became acknowledged by the entire pantheon. Since Marduk was the god of Babylon, this myth sought to convince the world that Babylon was the supreme nation, as it worshiped the supreme god. A similar development took place in Assyria where Asshur was acknowledged as the supreme god. The worship of Marduk or Asshur did not lessen the importance of the other deities, however. It seems illogical to us, but the temples and shrines of the pantheon were as busy as ever. The only change was in the new honors due to Marduk. Polytheism can be very tolerant, and the Babylonians did not strive after logic in their religion.

A faithful son of Ishtar, the mother goddess, bore the name Tammuz, Sumerian *Dumu-zi,* "faithful son." Tammuz was a god of vegetation who disappeared each year in the late summer and returned (i.e., was resurrected) the following spring. Tammuz was the suffering god whose career paralleled the natural seasons. With the deadly summer heat he left the earth, but the life-giving springtime saw his triumphant return. In the Greco-Roman world he was worshiped as Adonis, a name which is a variant of the Semitic *Adon,* lord, or master.

In addition to the great gods of the Babylonian pantheon, each individual of latter-day Babylon looked to a personal god who was thought to be his protector and provider — a kind of "guardian angel" who never left his charge except when the person was guilty of grievous sin. In the early stages of Assyrian and Babylonian thought, the king alone was the favorite of a special deity, but by the beginnings of the Old Babylonian Empire this distinction was enjoyed by commoners as well. The faith of the Babylonian in his personal gods is exemplified by names which individuals bore. We meet people who bear names meaning: "My god hath hearkened unto me," "My god is my father," "My god is my refuge."

The colossal winged bulls which guarded the approaches to Assyrian and Babylonian palaces were not solely decorative. They exemplified the good genies, or spirits, and served as guards for the protection of palaces or city gates. They had their counterpart, however, in the evil genies who sought to bring harm to mankind.

The evil genies were thought to be responsible for the strife which enters human relations. They entered houses even when the door was bolted and barred. They set family members at strife with one another. They might turn everything in the house upside down, enter the stable and injure or kill the animals. If they found a man in sin without the protection of his personal god, they might enter that man and "possess" him. The man could not escape this evil genie, for the records assure us, "The man who hath not god as he walketh in the street, the demon covers him as a garment."

The origin of the genies is somewhat obscure. The good ones, fewer in number, were descended from the great gods who continued to be worshiped in Babylon. The evil genies, however, were traced back to the evil gods whom Marduk destroyed in order to free the other gods from the evil which they purposed. At times the evil genies were described as children of Bel or Anu, although their mother was thought to be a goddess of the nether regions. On occasion, however, even the offspring of good gods such as Ea and his wife Damkina might become evil genies.

In addition to the offspring of the gods, whom we have called genies, the Babylonian felt himself surrounded by ghosts, or spirits of men whose lives had proved unhappy on earth. The ghosts had been cheated out of happiness in this life. Some of them had died violent deaths. All experienced what we term frustration. Nursing their grief, they were determined to torment the living.

12

THE BABYLONIAN PRIESTHOOD

In ancient Babylon the king served as both High Priest and civil ruler. He performed sacrifices and determined the religious life of his subjects. Since the king could not personally officiate in each of the temples in his realm, he appointed substitute priests to perform the routine priestly labors. Each temple would have a high priest, appointed by the king, and a number of lesser priests, known as *shangu,* who were also responsible to the king. The temple affairs were administered by these men who were chosen because of their fitness for the work.

There were other priestly functions of a specialized nature which presupposed specific training. The task of divination, the interpreting of dreams, and otherwise determining the will of the gods, was entrusted to the *buru* priests. The interpretation of oracles and dreams was on the basis of a long tradition of divination which the *buru* priest was expected to master. Hepatoscopy, or divination by the liver, was an ancient method of divination used by Hittites and Etruscans as well as by the Babylonians. The liver was regarded as the seat of the mental life. At the time of sacrifice, a god was thought to take hold of the victim, and the god's thoughts were presumed to enter the animal's liver. After a kid or sheep was slaughtered sacrificially, the victim's body was opened and preliminary conclusions drawn. Then the liver was removed and subjected to careful examination. Actual livers were compared with terra-cotta models and abnormalities were noted. We do not know how various configurations were interpreted but we know that ancient kings and their officers had a high regard for divination by the liver.[1]

Hittites and Etruscans, in common with Babylonians, also studied the flight patterns of birds as a means of divination. We

1. Divination by liver was one means used by Nebuchadnezzar in determining whether to attack Jerusalem or Rabbath Ammon (Ezek. 21:18-23).

do not know exactly what they looked for, but diviners skilled
in this type of divination regularly accompanied the armies of
Babylon.

Babylon was noted for its astrology, but this differed in important particulars from the astrology which developed in medie-
val times, based on Greek antecedents. Babylonian astrologers
noted the direction of the winds, the color of the stars, and the
occultation of planets and eclipses. The information provided by
Babylonian astrologers was used in agriculture as well as in matters of national policy.[2]

The Babylonian priests were constantly on the lookout for the
abnormal. Any unusual circumstance attending a birth, human
or animal, would be considered a sign which needed interpretation. If an exorcist were called to the home of an invalid, everything which he encountered along the way would be considered
significant. If water were spilled on the road, its pattern might
contain a message. The shape of oil which had formed on the
surface of water would be duly noted. If an animal or plant were
encountered, its significance would require interpretation.

To the Babylonian with his world of gods and demons it was
particularly important to have means of frustrating the forces of
evil. A class of priests known as *ashipu* specialized in counteracting the work of demons. A formula used in one of their spells
runs:

> Thou art not to come near to my body,
> Thou art not to go before me,
> Thou art not to follow after me,
> Where I stop thou art not to stop,
> Where I am thou art not to sit,
> My house thou art not to enter,
> My roof thou art not to haunt,
> Thou art not to put thy foot in my foot's imprint,
> Where I go thou art not to go,
> Where I enter thou art not to enter.[3]

The purpose of the *ashipu* was always benevolent. He sought
to help the sufferer who was physically ill, and in this sense his
work anticipates the physician. All sickness was associated with
sin in Babylonian thought, so the *ashipu* sought to discover what
sin had been committed by his "patient." A list of possible sins
would be read with the thought that one of them might have
been committed unconsciously. Only when the proper sin had
been identified could the *ashipu* overcome the demon that had
controlled the individual.

---

2. See p. 69.
3. G. Contenau, *La magie chez les Assyriens et les Babyloniens*, p. 147.

Sometimes demons were induced to leave their victims on the basis of a promise that the *ashipu* would give. A substitute habitation (such as a pig) was sometimes offered. At other times the demon might be bribed with a list of gifts that would be his as a reward for leaving his victim.

Another technique was to drive the demon from his victim. This might be done by preparing medicines of nauseous and putrid substances which the victim was required to eat. Presumably, if they were vile enough, the demon himself would not wish to remain. Eventually, by the process of trial and error, some substances were employed which had genuine medicinal value. Thus medicine, although mixed with magic, became a genuine science.

Sometimes demons could be fooled. One recognized means of doing this was by placing an animal on top of a sick man. By following a prescribed ritual, the demon might be persuaded to enter the animal instead of the human. One such prescription reads:

> Take a sucking-pig and set it level with the head of the sick man. Take out its heart and put it over the sick man's heart. Sprinkle the sides of the bed with its blood. Dismember the sucking-pig and lay the parts on the sick man's members. Then purify this man with pure water... Offer the sucking-pig in his place. Let its flesh be as the flesh of the sick man, his blood as the blood of the sick man.[4]

The *ashipu* priest was clothed in red when performing his functions. Red was deemed particularly potent in warding off evil spirits. He might also be dressed in a fish-like skin to emphasize his relationship to the wise god, Ea. Traditional formulae were uttered verbatim. The priest would call upon the demon by name, demanding that he cease tormenting his victim and depart. Calling upon the good gods to aid the sufferer, the *ashipu* priest would exorcise the demon.

Another specialized functionary was the chanter who, by his songs, was supposed to "soften the heart of the gods." Prayers were intoned by the chanters, who were accompanied by large drums or lyres. The lyre was usually decorated with a bull's head, and the tone itself was likened to the bellowing of a bull. Of the ancient Babylonian chants which we possess, fifty-seven require the accompaniment of a drum, forty require a flute, and forty-seven involve the "lifting of hands" in the attitude of prayer.

The Book of Daniel gives us a Biblical picture of the Babylonian priests and wise men at work. Diviners claimed to have existed as a separate order from remote antiquity, and it was required that they be physically sound. Daniel and his companions are

---

4. G. Contenau, *op. cit.*, p. 225.

described as "children in whom was no blemish" (Dan. 1:4).
The Babylonian texts insist: "the diviner whose father is impure
and who himself has any imperfection of limb or countenance,
whose eyes are not sound, who has any teeth missing, who has lost
a finger, whose countenance has a sickly look or who is pimpled,
cannot be the keeper of the decrees of Shamash and Adad."[5]

Those who purposed to be Babylonian diviners were required
to take a long course of study before they could serve at the
Babylonian court. The Hebrew captives were subjected to a
three year training program in "the learning and the tongue of
the Chaldeans" (Dan. 1:4-5) after which they were given court
appointments. It is evident that Babylonians were receiving the
same schooling, for we are told that Daniel and his friends were
"ten times better than all the magicians and astrologers" (Dan.
1:20). When the wise men of Babylon were unable to interpret
the dream of Nebuchadnezzar we are told that Daniel did so,
after which the king placed him "over all the wise men of Babylon" (Dan. 2:48).

The Book of Daniel makes it clear that diviners were expected
to be able to interpret anything, and that they formed an important element in the king's court. The godly Daniel, however,
humbly trusting his God, showed Nebuchadnezzar that the magic
and sorcery of Babylon could not be trusted to meet the basic
problems of men or nations.

---

5. G. Contenau, *Everyday Life in Babylon and Assyria*, p. 281.

13

BABYLON'S LAST KINGS

The Babylonian Empire reached its zenith under Nebuchadnezzar and, twenty-three years after his death, its capital city fell before Cyrus of Anshan, the founder of the Persian Empire. Three rather unpretentious and largely ineffective rulers governed Babylon during that scant quarter century.

1. Amel Marduk (562-560 B.C.)

At the death of Nebuchadnezzar his throne was taken at once by Amel Marduk, the Evil-merodach ("man of Marduk") of Scripture. He is known to Bible students as the kindly Babylonian ruler who released Jehoiachin from prison during the thirty-seventh year after his captivity and provided him with suitable garments and meals — appropriate for his royal station (II Kings 25:27-30). Berossus, however, describes Amel Marduk as a tyrannical ruler who despised the laws of his people.[1] It may be that his attitude toward Jehoiachin and other captives proved offensive to Babylonian rulers who felt that he had set aside the policies of Nebuchadnezzar in favor of an independent course of action. In any event, he was assassinated during the second year of his reign by his sister's husband, Neriglissar, who usurped the throne.

The French archaeologist, De Morgan, while excavating Susa, in Persia, discovered a vase which had been taken from Babylon to Persia in ancient times. It bore an inscription which read, "Palace of Amel-Marduk, King of Babylon, son of Nebuchadnezzar, King of Babylon."[2]

---

1. Berossus, Frag. 14, in C. Müller, *Fragmenta Historicorum Graecorum*, II p. 507.
2. George A. Barton, *Archaeology and the Bible*, p. 479.

2. Neriglissar (Nergal-shar-usur) (560-556 B.C.)

It is probable that Neriglissar was a leading prince in the Babylonian court long before he seized the throne. A man of that name entered Jerusalem with the armies of Nebuchadnezzar and held the post of Rab-mag with the occupying armies (Jer. 39:3). The meaning of Rab-mag (Akkadian *rab-mugi*) is uncertain but it designates a high political office. Nergal-shar-usur was one of "the princes of the king of Babylon" and he sat "in the middle gate" of Jerusalem, which evidently served as the center of government for the Babylonians before they destroyed the city. Nergal-shar-usur as Rab-mag was a member of the delegation assigned to release Jeremiah from prison and entrust him into the friendly hands of Gedaliah (Jer. 39:11-14). He had married a daughter of Nebuchadnezzar and, for that reason, considered himself a legitimate successor to his throne.

Neriglissar took pride in the adornment of Babylon and the beautifying of its temples. As a practical consideration he regulated the course of the canal upon which the city of Babylon was built. This was a channel of the Euphrates, but it was altered to permit it to pass by the E-sag-ila temple. The eastern arm of the canal was walled up so that its current might flow with sweet water, unmixed with sand.

Neriglissar also repaired his palace, which had earlier been the residence of Nebuchadnezzar. Its foundations were strengthened and a lofty summit was added to the structure, made of brick, the usual building material of Mesopotamia, and expensive cedar beams imported from Lebanon.

We know of no wars during the reign of Neriglissar. The Empire was preserved intact and the four years of his reign appear to have been prosperous ones. He died a natural death, albeit in the very prime of life. His son, Labashi-Marduk was named his successor, but after a reign of but nine months he was murdered and a successor, satisfactory to the priestly party, was chosen to serve as king.

3. Nabonidus (Nabu-na'id) (556-539 B.C.)

After the murder of Labashi-Marduk, the priestly party in Babylon chose as king Nabonidus, the son of Nabu-balatsu-iqbi, a man who had distinguished himself both in the affairs of state and church. His chief energies seem to have been extended in building and restoring temples.

Nabonidus was thorough in his work. In rebuilding a temple he was not content merely to level off the ground and make a fresh beginning. Nabonidus searched diligently until he found the original foundation stone. Then he could read the name of the king who first ordered the construction of the temple. In this way both a religious and an antiquarian interest were served, for Nabonidus could have his royal scribes determine the number of years which had passed since the temple foundations were first laid. Such lists are invaluable to students of ancient Near Eastern history. A daughter of Nabonidus is said to have maintained a small museum of archaeological finds. Another, Bel-shalti-nannar, served as a priestess in the famed temple to the moon god at Ur which her father had restored.

In building inscriptions left by Nabonidus he designates himself as "Preserver of E-sag-ila and E-zida" the great shrines of the city of Babylon. Actually the chief interest of Nabonidus was not in these shrines and he incurred the anger of his priests for neglecting the annual visit to the E-sag-ila shrine which every Babylonian king was expected to make on the New Year's Day.

Year after year he remained at Tema, according to the Nabunaid Chronicle. The records bear the disquieting note, "The king did not come to Babylon for the ceremonies of the month Nisanu, Nabu did not come to Babylon, Bel did not go out from E-sag-ila in procession, the festival of the New Year was omitted." The Babylonian priests considered Nabonidus guilty of sacrilege in failing to take the hand of Marduk at the New Year's festival. This rite was thought to convey ceremonially the right to rule for the ensuing year.

While neglecting the shrines of Babylon, Nabonidus found satisfaction in such activities as the rebuilding of the temple to the sun god at ancient Sippar. Nebuchadnezzar had rebuilt this structure forty-five years earlier, but it had already fallen into disrepair. After providing temporary quarters for Shamash, the sun god, Nabonidus ordered the temple razed. Then he searched for the original foundation which was far below the surface of the ground. It had been laid by Naram-Sin, a king of the Akkad Dynasty (*ca.* 2360-2180 B.C.), who had ruled seventeen hundred years before Nabonidus!

Nabonidus was delighted with the find, asserting that Shamash himself had shown the foundation stone to him. On the exact site of the old sanctuary, Nabonidus built the new temple, E-babbara. He spared no expense. Five thousand cedar beams were imported for its roof, and more of the wood was required for its great doors. When completed, Nabonidus conducted the god Shamash into his new temple with prayers that the god might honor and protect the king who had provided this new temple for him.

Another shrine at Sippar, E-ulmash, the temple of Anunitum, was rebuilt by Nabonidus at about the same time as the E-bab-bara. Even more ambitious was his concern for E-khulkhul, the shrine of Sin, the moon god, at the ancient city of Haran in northern Mesopotamia. Haran had been devoted to the same god as the city of Ur, in southern Mesopotamia, and the patriarchal family sojourned there en route to Canaan.

During the first year of his reign, Nabonidus dreamed a dream in which he received a command: "Nabonidus, king of Babylon, on thy cart-horses bring bricks, build E-khulkhul, and let Sin, the great lord, take up his residence within it."[3] Nabonidus objected that the temple was surrounded by the Manda, a generic term for the northern barbarians. It may refer here either to Medes or Scythians. The oracle assured Nabonidus that the Manda were no longer in the vicinity of Haran, and that it would therefore be safe for Nabonidus to enter the city. This episode tells a great deal about the character of Nabonidus. One of the Assyrian rulers would have marched his armies against the Manda and stormed their city. Nabonidus, however, was strictly a man of peaceful pursuits.

Men and materials were gathered from the entire Babylonian Empire. Great new walls, which Nabonidus assures us were stronger than the earlier ones, soon arose. Again, as for the temple for Shamash, cedar was used for the roof and the doors. Sin and his companions (the lesser gods) were escorted into the new temple amidst pomp and splendor.

The religious and antiquarian interests of Nabonidus might have appeared innocent enough had he given due attention to the affairs of state, but this was his prime weakness. He chose to live at Tema, an oasis in the Hejaz region of Arabia. Recognizing the need of someone to care for the more prosaic affairs of state, he appointed his son Belshazzar (Bel-shar-usur) as co-regent.

The Verse Account of Nabonidus tells of his expedition to Tema:

> He entrusted the "Camp" to his oldest son, the first-born
> The troops everywhere in the country he ordered under his
> command.

---

3. T. Fish, "Texts Relating to Nabonidus," in D. Winston Thomas, *Documents from Old Testament Times*, p. 89.

> He let everything go, entrusted the kingship to him
> And, himself, he started out for a long journey,
> The military forces of Akkad marching with him;
> He turned toward Tema, deep in the west.
> He started out the expedition on a path leading to a
>   distant region. When he arrived there,
> He killed in battle the prince of Tema,
> Slaughtered the flocks of those who dwell in the city
>   as well as in the countryside
> And he, himself, took his residence in Tema, the forces
>   of Akkad were also stationed there.
> He made the town beautiful, built there his palace
> Like the palace in Babylon, he also built walls
> For the fortifications of the town and . . .
> He surrounded the town with sentinels 4

Among the Qumran discoveries is a document known as the Prayer of Nabonidus which was published in 1956 by J. T. Milik.[5] The document begins: "The words of the prayer which Nabonidus, king of Assyria and Babylon, the great king, prayed . . . ." It tells how Nabonidus came down with a "dread disease by the decree of the Most High God." Therefore he was "set apart from men" for seven years in the Arabian Oasis of Tema. An unnamed Jewish diviner appeared to remind the king of his idolatry in worshiping "gods of gold, bronze, iron, wood, stone, silver . . . ."

This episode is reminiscent of the account of the humbling of Nebuchadnezzar in Daniel 4. Nebuchadnezzar, while boasting about his accomplishments as king in Babylon, was stricken by a divine judgment and became insane. He lived like an animal until seven "times" (probably years) had passed, after which he acknowledged the sovereignty of the Most High and was restored to his throne. It is the view of some scholars that the events described in Daniel 4 actually took place during the lifetime of Nabonidus and that a scribal error associated them with the more familiar name of Nebuchadnezzar.[6]

4. Belshazzar

Belshazzar was co-regent with Nabonidus from the third year

4. A. Leo Oppenheim, "Babylonian and Assyrian Historical Texts," in James Pritchard, *Ancient Near Eastern Texts,* pp. 313-314.
5. "Priere de Nabonide' et autres ecrits d'un cycle de Daniel," *Revue Biblique* 63 (1956), pp. 407-15.
6. The suggestion of a copyist's error is given in the *Catholic Biblical Encyclopedia* (Edited by John E. Steinmueller and Kathryn Sullivan), p. 145. Others suggest that the tradition associated with the name of Nabonidus was erroneously ascribed to Nebuchadnezzar. See: David Noel Freedman, "The Prayer of Nabonidus," *Bulletin of the American Schools of Oriental Research,* No. 145 (1957), pp. 31-32.

of his reign. Nabonidus never abdicated his throne, but for all practical purposes Belshazzar served as king. In the cuneiform documents Belshazzar is consistently called "the son of the king." Texts from the fifth to the thirteenth years of the reign of Nabonidus speak of offerings of silver, gold, and sacrificial animals which Belshazzar made to Babylonian temples.

Belshazzar did not make a strong ruler. He is best known for his impious feast, described in the fifth chapter of the Book of Daniel, which was going on while the Persian armies were approaching Babylon. Belshazzar was in Babylon when it fell to the armies of Cyrus. Although the city fell without a battle, Belshazzar himself was slain.

14

DANIEL OF BABYLON

Daniel was a young man of noble descent and high physical and intellectual endowments when Jehoiakim came to the throne of Judah. He was probably born during the reign of Josiah, and his home appears to have been one in which the Law of the Lord was honored. During the years when idolatry ran rampant, following Josiah's death, Daniel was to form the attitudes of faithfulness to his God which would help him to meet the later temptations of idolatrous Babylon. In Daniel's youth he learned of the fall of Nineveh, a fact which changed the course of history and made the Babylonians the new masters of western Asia.

The Book of Daniel tells us that Nebuchadnezzar of Babylon besieged Jerusalem during the third year of Jehoiakim's reign. The siege was successful, and Jehoiakim gave the Babylonian king temple treasures which were taken to Babylon. More important, however, was the fact that Nebuchadnezzar ordered that a number of young men of good families who were physically strong and intellectually of high calibre, be transported to Babylon where they might serve him in an official capacity. This was an act of wisdom on Nebuchadnezzar's part. Taking the best youths of Jerusalem would weaken the state of Judah, and thus reduce its potential for rebellion. If he could win the loyalty of these young men, Babylon itself would be the stronger for their presence.

The treatment accorded Daniel and his companions who were taken to Babylon at Nebuchadnezzar's command, is comparable to modern techniques of "brain washing." These lads were not subjected to torture. They were, instead, given every encouragement to forget past loyalties and become well integrated Babylonians.

The names which the Judaean lads bore were indicative of their Jewish origin. Daniel means, "God is my judge." His three companions bore names meaning, "Yahweh is gracious," (Hananiah) ; "Who is what God is?" (Mishael), and "Yahweh has helped" (Azariah). In each instance the Babylonian substitute name removed the reference to Israel's God —El (Elohim), or Yahweh (Dan. 1:7).

Daniel became Belteshazzar, a name which appears in Babylonian documents as Balatsu-usur ("Protect his life!"). Hananiah became Shadrach (perhaps Shadur-Aku, "the command of Aku" a name for the Babylonian moon god). Shadrach may be an intentional corruption of the name of Marduk, the chief god of Babylon. Mishael's Babylonian name, Meshach, seems to correspond to his Hebrew name. Babylonian Meshach may mean "Who is what Aku is?" although scholars are not certain of its derivation. Azariah's Babylonian name, Abed-nego, however, follows a common pattern in Semitic languages. A man is considered to be a servant of his god, hence the term "servant" is common in Semitic names. Abed-nego means "servant of Nego," a corruption of "servant of Nebo," the popular Babylonian god whose name appears in that of the king Nebuchadnezzar (Babylonian, Nabu-kudurru-usur, "Nabu, establish the boundary!"). The Scriptures contain several names which are compounds of *abed*: Obadiah "Servant of Yahweh," and Ebed-melech, "Servant of (the god) Melech." The term "servant" or "slave" speaks of one who is a worshiper of his deity. The common Moslem name Abdullah ("slave [or worshiper] of Allah") is based on the same pattern.

The assigning of new names to people who enter new cultural (and, particularly, political) situations was relatively common in the ancient world. Joseph, in Egypt, was assigned the name Zaphnath-paaneah (Gen. 41:45). Other Jews in Babylon bore such distinctly pagan names as Zer-Babili (Zerubbabel), "the seed of Babylon," and Marduka (Mordecai), the name of the god of Babylon. It is significant that the Hebrew youths did not make an issue of the change in name imposed upon them. Usually, however, the Book of Daniel refers to them by their Jewish names.

An important element in the preparation of the youths for service to Babylon was the training program in which they were enrolled. At the time of choosing suitable youths for Nebuchadnezzar's purposes it was determined that they must be "skilful in all wisdom, endowed with knowledge, understanding, learning." It was the king's purpose "to teach them the letters and language of the Chaldeans" (Dan. 1:4).

Preliminary to studying the religion, science, and cultural traditions of the Babylonian people, Daniel and his companions had to learn to read and write the language which we now term Akkadian. This was written in cuneiform characters impressed on clay tablets. These hundreds of signs, in part pictographs and in part syllables, had been in use since Sumerian times.[1]

A third part of the acculturation of the Hebrew youths was in the matter of diet, for: "the king assigned them a daily portion of the rich food which the king ate, and of the wine which he drank" (Dan. 1:5). From the Babylonian viewpoint this was a gracious act. Captive youths had come from many places, and the living standards of most would be far inferior to that of Babylon. They should be grateful for such treatment as the king now provided. They would enjoy meals truly "fit for a king."

Yet, strange as it may seem to us, it is precisely here that Daniel and his companions drew the line. The names and the schooling were accepted in good grace, but "Daniel resolved that he would not defile himself" (Dan. 1:8) in the matter of eating the king's food. The Law of Moses contained explicit commands concerning clean and unclean foods, and Daniel knew that the Babylonian kitchens cared nothing for the Levitical regulations. The gods of Babylon would be invoked at these Babylonian festivities, and Daniel could not conscientiously take part in them.

The manner in which Daniel sought release from the obligation to eat the royal meals explains in part his effectiveness in a heathen court. Daniel quietly approached the steward who was responsible for the care of the lads. He suggested a ten day testing period during which a vegetable diet might be eaten and water drunk (Dan. 1:11-13). The four youths would then be examined by the steward who could determine for himself if they were physically weaker than those who ate the royal dainties. When the time came, Daniel and his friends were found to be "better in appearance and fatter in flesh" than those who had eaten the meals provided by the king (Dan. 1:15).) The steward being convinced that it was safe to permit the Hebrew lads to continue their vegetable diet, the pressure to conform was relieved. During the three year training period the young men were not molested again.

When Nebuchadnezzar dreamed, and forgot his dream, none of the wise men of Babylon could help him (Dan. 2:1-11). It was Daniel who, under God, was able to tell Nebuchadnezzar

---

1. See Chapter 10.

both the dream and its interpretation (Dan. 2:12-45). Nebuchadnezzar had seen a large image, the parts of which were made
of different metals: "The head of this image was of fine gold, its
breast and arms of silver, its belly and thighs of bronze, its legs
of iron, its feet partly of iron and partly of clay" (Dan. 2:32-33).
A stone struck the top-heavy image, totally destroying it. The
stone, however, grew until it filled the whole earth.

In interpreting the dream, Daniel told the king that the image
represented a series of world powers. The head of gold represented Nebuchadnezzar and his Babylonian kingdom. Babylon
would be succeeded by three kings, becoming successively inferior. At the close of this period of world empire, "the God of heav-
en will set up a kingdom which shall never be destroyed, nor
shall its sovereignty be left to another people" (Dan. 2:44). Daniel clearly asserts that God is to have the last word on the human
scene, and that Nebuchadnezzar and all that should follow him
indulged in a transient glory.

The king recognized his dream, and honored Daniel for his
ability in interpreting it. Daniel was made governor of the province of Babylon and chief prefect over the wise men of the
land. He occupied a place at the royal court (Dan. 2:48-49). The
king also honored Daniel's God, recognizing that He had enabled
Daniel to become the interpreter of the dream (Dan. 2:46-47).

Nebuchadnezzar saw in a second dream a great tree which
reached to heaven. The tree was then cut down with only its
stump remaining. This was bound with a band of iron and left
with the grass of the field. A second time Daniel was able to interpret the king's dream. The great tree was Nebuchadnezzar
himself. As the tree was cut down, so Daniel assured the king
that he would be humbled. Daniel predicted that Nebuchadnezzar would become insane and live like the beasts of the field until
he would give due glory to God (Dan. 4:1-27). A year later, as
Nebuchadnezzar was boasting about his accomplishments,[2] Daniel's interpretation of the dream proved correct. Nebuchadnezzar
"ate grass like an ox, and his body was wet with the dew of heav-
en till his hair grew as long as eagles' feathers, and his nails were
like birds' claws" (Dan. 4:33). His insanity continued until he
ascribed glory to the Most High (Dan. 4:34-35). Then his reason
returned and he honored the God of Daniel as King of Heaven
(Dan. 4:37).

2. See Chapter 9; Daniel 4:30.

We read no more of Daniel until the reign of Belshazzar.[3] As the Persians were marching upon Babylon, Belshazzar prepared a great feast for his loyal courtiers. In his impiety, the king drank wine from the very vessels which had once been used in the Temple at Jerusalem (Dan. 5:3). Suddenly God spoke in judgment. The fingers of a hand were visible at the wall of the chamber. They wrote an inscription on the plaster and Belshazzar was terrified. As in the days of Nebuchadnezzar, the wise men of the realm were called in but they were unable to decipher the strange writing. Remembering that Daniel had shown supernatural wisdom in the days of Nebuchadnezzar, the queen suggested that he be asked to read and interpret the mysterious writing. Daniel, spurning any idea of reward, reminded Belshazzar of the way in which Nebuchadnezzar had been humbled by God (Dan. 5:17-21). Belshazzar had not profited by his knowledge of God's dealings with Nebuchadnezzar, but instead had defied the Lord (Dan. 5:22-23).

Daniel read the words on the palace wall: Mene, Mene, Tekel, and Parsin. These words could represent Babylonian weights — "a mana, a mana, a shekel, and a half-shekel." They also could be interpreted as verbs — "numbered, numbered, weighed, and divided." It was in the latter sense that Daniel interpreted the words. The days of Belshazzar's kingdom were *numbered*. He was *weighed* in the balances and found wanting. His kingdom was *divided* and given to the Medes and Persians (Dan. 5:25-28). The word "Peres" (singular of *parsin*) would also bring to mind the Persians whose kingdom would supplant that of the Babylonians.

On that very night the Persian armies entered the city of Babylon. Belshazzar was slain and the Neo-Babylonian Empire was at an end. The city of Babylon was not destroyed, however. Cyrus was soon to enter the city and be proclaimed as its deliverer from the misrule of Nabonidus and Belshazzar.[4]

Daniel was not a minister to the people, as was Ezekiel, but he did represent the claims of Israel's God before the Babylonian court. His efficient service and his pious example proved an effective testimony. The Persian conquerers preserved much of the governmental structure of their predecessors, and Daniel appears to have continued his official tasks (Dan. 6:1-4). The other officials grew jealous of the power vested in Daniel and determined

3. See pp. 87-88.
4. See p. 103.

to get rid of him. They knew that he was faithful in his official functions, so they contrived a plot to have him killed on religious grounds. They appealed to the Persian ruler, Darius[5] suggesting that he issue an edict forbidding prayers to any but the king for a thirty day period (Dan. 6:6-9). Any who would presume to disobey would be cast into a den of lions.

As they expected, Daniel paid no attention to the edict. Regularly, three times a day, he turned toward Jerusalem in prayer (Dan. 6:10). Darius was unhappy at the thought of casting his faithful courtier to the lions, but the edict could not be changed (Dan. 6:14). Daniel did not flinch. He was cast to the lions, but Darius seems to have spent more of a restless night than he (Dan. 6:18). God protected his faithful servant and, the next morning, his accusers were cast to the lions (Dan. 6:19-24). Darius, like Nebuchadnezzar, honored the God of Daniel (Dan. 6:25-28).

We know nothing about the close of Daniel's life. He lived through the entire period of the Exile and, while he did not return to Jerusalem, it was uppermost in his thoughts. He studied the prophecies of Jeremiah (Dan. 9:2) and prayed that God might restore the people to their city: "O my God, incline thy ear and hear; open thy eyes and behold our desolations, and the city which is called by thy name; for we do not present our supplications before thee on the ground of our righteousness, but on the ground of thy great mercy. O Lord, hear; O Lord, forgive, give heed and act; delay not, for thy own sake, O my God, because thy city and thy people are called by thy name" (Dan. 9:18-19).

---

5. The identity of "Darius the Mede" is a vexing historical problem. See John C. Whitcomb, *Darius the Mede,* for a proposed solution.

15

EZEKIEL AND THE EXILES

The great prophetic figure in Babylon during the Exile was Ezekiel, the son of Buzi, a priest who had been deported at the time of Jehoiachin's captivity, eleven years before the destruction of Jerusalem (II Kings 24:12-15). Ezekiel prophesied in Babylon during the years when Jeremiah was uttering God's message to Judah in Jerusalem. The two prophets declared essentially the same truths, but their backgrounds as well as their environment give each a peculiar cast.

As a young man, Ezekiel may have actually ministered in the Jerusalem Temple. He certainly mastered both the ritual and moral law of Israel, and was thoroughly familiar with all of the priestly duties of his office. As a student of Torah, the "Law" or "instruction" in the widest sense, Ezekiel also came to know the history of his people. He studied about the call of the patriarchs, the deliverance from Egypt, the giving of the Law through Moses and the establishment of Israel in Canaan as evidence of the mighty power of God on behalf of His people. Ezekiel was certainly conscious of the many apostasies of Israel, and of the great prophets — men such as Elijah — raised up of God to call His people back from their evil ways. Ezekiel probably had a first-hand knowledge of the teaching of Jeremiah, his older contemporary. He was sympathetic with the great revival under King Josiah, with its implications for his priestly ministry. Ezekiel, like Jeremiah, mourned because of the idolatry of Israel as it was ripe for exile.

Ezekiel's training and priestly service came to an end in 597 B.C. when he was taken to Babylon along with many other talented youths from Judah. Scripture gives us no hint of his age at the time of the exile, Josephus[1] says that he was a boy, but this

---

1. Josephus, *Antiquities*, **X**, vii, 3.

Kefil. Although there is no record of the death of Ezekiel, or of the location of his grave, tradition suggests that he died in Babylon during the reign of Nebuchadnezzar and that he was buried at Kefil, near Babylon, between the Chebar and the Euphrates.

Courtesy, Matson Photo Service

is probably a guess. He may have been thirty years of age at the time, or even older. Neither the record in II Kings 24:10-16 nor the Book of Ezekiel mentions priests among those deported with Jehoiachin. Ezekiel was probably taken because of his high reputation among the priests. He must have impressed his contemporaries as a man of uncommon ability, and it was that type of individual that Nebuchadnezzar took into exile.

In Babylon, Ezekiel settled with his fellow countrymen in a community named Tel-abib along the River Chebar, a short distance southeast of Babylon. From an incidental allusion (Ezek. 8:1) we learn that he was married and had a house of his own. His wife was suddenly taken from him (Ezek. 24:18). Since she is termed the delight of his eyes (Ezek. 24:16) we may assume that his marriage was a happy one and that the death of his wife brought genuine grief to the prophet. He used the occasion to warn his countrymen that God was about to bring judgment upon their Temple and their loved ones.

Five years after his deportation, Ezekiel saw a remarkable vision of the glory of the Lord (Ezek. 1), after which he received a commission to bring God's Word to the rebellious house of Israel (Ezek. 2). He ate the scroll which was offered to him, and found it sweet (Ezek. 3:1-3). Led by the Spirit, he went to Tel-abib where he remained in silence for seven days (Ezek. 3:12-15). Reminded that he was responsible to God as a watchman of His people (Ezek. 3:16-21), he there began his active ministry.

Ezekiel was directed to draw the city plan of Jerusalem on a brick[2] and make an iron plate to serve as its wall. This mock city was to be besieged in a realistic way. Ezekiel was told to build a tower, throw up a mound, establish camps, and set battering rams around it (Ezek. 4:1-3). Then the prophet was instructed to lie on his left side for three hundred and ninety days to symbolically bear the punishment of the house of Israel, and forty days to bear Judah's punishment (Ezek. 4:4-8). Each day was to represent a year of punishment for Israel and Judah because of their sin. Food and water were to be measured as a reminder that siege conditions would prevail in Jerusalem (Ezek. 4:9-17).

The prophet was next instructed to shave his head and beard and weigh the hair in a balance. A third he burned in the city; a third he struck with the sword outside the city walls; and a third he scattered to the winds. A remnant he bound in his garment,

---

2. This would be a clay tablet such as was used for writing. A map of the world as known to the ancient Babylonians appears on such a tablet.

only to throw part into the fire. This symbolic act portrayed the future of Jerusalem: "A third part of you shall die of pestilence and be consumed with famine in the midst of you; a third part shall fall by the sword round about you; and a third part I will scatter to all the winds and will unsheathe the sword after them" (Ezek. 5:12).

The following year Ezekiel was taken in spirit to Jerusalem where, at the north gate of the inner Temple court, he was shown the "image of jealousy" which provoked the wrath of God (Ezek. 8:1-6). It derived its name from the fact that it served as a challenge to the rights of the Lord over his people. In the Law, Israel's God declared Himself to be "a jealous God" (Exod. 20:5), and insisted that no image of any kind should receive worship. God said to Ezekiel, " 'Son of man, lift up your eyes now in the direction of the north'. So I lifted up my eyes toward the north, and behold, north of this altar gate, in the entrance, was this image of jealousy. And he said to me, 'Son of man, do you see what they are doing, the great abominations that the house of Israel are committing here to drive me far from my sanctuary?' " (Ezek. 8:5-6). God did not wish to leave His people. He was being driven away!

Ezekiel was next taken to the Temple wall and ordered to dig. He found a hidden door which opened into a secret room, the walls of which were decorated with serpents and wild beasts (Ezek. 8:7-10). The description is reminiscent of the walls along the famed Procession Way in the city of Babylon, adorned with lions, bulls, and dragons.[3] Seventy elders were inside the room burning incense in an idolatrous ritual (Ezek 8:11-13).

At the north gate of the Temple, Ezekiel saw more evidence of idolatry. The women were weeping for Tammuz,[4] the Babylonian vegetation deity whose death was mourned each year by his worshipers (Ezek. 8:14-15). The worst scandal of all was at the Temple entrance. There Ezekiel saw about twenty-five Jerusalemites with their backs to the Temple, facing eastward as they adored the sun god[5] (Ezek. 8:16).

In Ezekiel's vision he saw swift judgment fall on the idolatrous city. God said, " ...I will deal in wrath; my eye will not spare nor will I have pity; and though they cry in my ears with a loud voice, I will not hear them" (Ezek. 8:18). Six executioners were

---

3. See p. 59.
4. See p. 77.
5. See p. 75.

dispatched into the city. Those who shared Ezekiel's sorrow over
the abominations of Jerusalem were given a special mark (Ezek.
9:4). All the others were slain (Ezek. 9:5-6). Finally, burning
coals were scattered over the doomed city (Ezek. 10:1-2).

Prophets and psalmists had long encouraged Israel to trust in
the God who is an ever present help. Ezekiel dared to say that
God would forsake Zion. In graphic language he told how God
would leave the Holy City. He described the departure of the
Shekinah glory cloud from the Holy of Holies in the Temple:
"And the glory of the Lord went up from the cherubim to the
threshold of the house; and the house was filled with the cloud,
and the court was full of the brightness of the glory of the Lord"
(Ezek. 10:4). God seemed to be reluctant to leave. He tarried
over the threshold as if to give the people an opportunity to
turn from their idols and live. Yet they did nothing to keep the
"glory" with them. From the threshold, cherubim lifted the glory
cloud to "the door of the east gate of the house of the Lord"
(Ezek. 10:18-19). Finally, "the glory of the Lord went up from
the midst of the city, and stood upon the mountain which is on
the east side of the city" (Ezek. 11:23). The glory had left the
Holy City! It was hovering over the Mount of Olives as though
still reluctant to depart.

The departure of the divine glory symbolized the departure
of God. The false prophets were right in insisting that the heath-
en could never take Jerusalem because God dwelt in the Temple
there. They were wrong in assuming that God would continue to
make His abode in the midst of a rebellious and idolatrous
people. When, six centuries later, another generation was to re-
ject the glory of God in the Person of Jesus Christ, He uttered
the fateful words, "Your house is left unto you, desolate" (Matt.
23:38). The Temple, without its God, is simply a house, and God
was in no way constrained to preserve its barren walls from the
enemy's ax.

By another symbol, Ezekiel translated the message of the de-
parting glory to his people. The prophet dug through the mud
brick wall of his house and brought out his personal property,
covering his head as he went so he could not see the ground. So,
Ezekiel intimated, the king of Judah would come as a captive to
Babylon, but he would not be able to see the land (Ezek.
12:1-13).

Such predictions would hardly make Ezekiel a popular man.
Although not subjected to the persecution which Jeremiah en-
dured, Ezekiel, like his counterpart in Jerusalem, found his mes-

sage opposed by the leaders of the community. Some may have admired Ezekiel's oratory, but few paid serious attention to his utterances. Like Jeremiah, Ezekiel was frequently opposed by false prophets who made optimistic predictions of a quick return from exile and the re-establishment of the Davidic throne in the person of Jehoiachin (Ezek. 13:1-10). From time to time the "elders of Judah" consulted Ezekiel, and his selfless identification with the people must have won him the respect of the spiritually discerning members of the community.

Following the destruction of Jerusalem (587 B.C.) we note a marked difference in Ezekiel's ministry. Before Jerusalem fell he could be characterized as the prophet of doom, categorically stating that the Holy City would be forsaken by God and destroyed by Nebuchadnezzar. Afterward, however, he emphasized the hope of a restored Jerusalem, with a restored Temple in which sacrifices would again be offered. It is in the closing chapters of his book that we note Ezekiel's priestly interest in the minutia of Temple worship.

During the latter period of his ministry, Ezekiel was probably given a more sympathetic hearing. His dire predictions had proved correct, and those who had entertained false hopes were now humbled. The fresh influx of exiles brought to Babylon following the destruction of Jerusalem probably included some who had been sympathetic with Jeremiah. They would be expected to rally around Ezekiel as a prophet in the same tradition as their former leader.

Ezekiel has been termed the architect of the restoration. The last eight chapters of his book describe the New Jerusalem of the restoration, the city which shall bear the name "The Lord is There" (Ezek. 48:35). From below the threshold of the Temple, Ezekiel sees waters gushing forth to bring refreshment to the entire land (Ezek. 47:1). Along the banks of the rivers he sees trees bearing fruit for food and leaves for healing (Ezek. 47:12).

The book of Ezekiel is difficult to fathom because of its rich imagery, some of which escapes us because of our removal in time and space from the world in which Ezekiel lived. Like Jeremiah, Ezekiel saw Babylon as the rod in God's hand to chasten rebellious Israel. He used all that he observed in drawing lessons for his people. The winged creatures of Babylonian art (Ezek. 1:8) formed the basis of his vision of the great chariot. Perhaps his knowledge of Babylonian temples as well as his recollection of the Jerusalem Sanctuary and the Scriptures which describe it formed the basis for his description of the Temple in the re-

stored Jerusalem. His long and accurate list of the natural resources and industrial products of different countries (Ezek. 27)
shows him to have been a man of broad experience.

Although interested in the restoration of national Israel, Ezekiel stresses the importance of the individual. He insisted that
"the son shall not suffer for the iniquity of the father, nor the
father suffer for the iniquity of the son" (Ezek. 18:20; 33:12). He
predicted judgment on sinful Israel, but also held forth the possibility of a heart of flesh which might replace the heart of stone.
He envisioned a new relationship for those who would be indeed
the people of God (Ezek. 11:19-20).

16

RETURN FROM EXILE

Nabonidus had not proved popular, and the expediency of appointing Belshazzar as co-regent had not helped matters. The Neo-Babylonian Empire might have struggled along for decades, or even centuries, were it not for the fact that an energetic young ruler from the Persian province of Anshan had dreams of conquest. Cyrus had incorporated Media into his own Persian domains and marched northward into Asia Minor. The Lydian Empire, ruled by the fabulously rich Croesus, was subdued, and it was obvious that Cyrus would soon turn back toward Babylon in his quest for even wider territorial expansion.

The Babylonian governor of Elam (Gutium) had deserted to Cyrus. The loss to Nabonidus was great. Elam was a large and influential province, and its governor, Gobryas, was an able general. Gobryas was soon leading sorties against Babylonia.

The religious innovations of Nabonidus had alienated him from many of his own people. Concern for foreign shrines, coupled with the neglect of the religious demands of his office, caused many of his own people to wish to be rid of him. He seems to have reinstituted the New Year Festival in April, 539 B.C., but it was too late by that time to reverse the trend which led to the downfall of his dynasty.[1]

By the summer of 539 B.C. the Persian armies were ready to attack Babylon. Nabonidus, sensing the situation, brought the gods of the outlying regions into his capital, trusting that they would aid him in his time of need! This only antagonized those whose gods were taken away and brought further resentment to the priests of Babylon.

The decisive battle was fought at Opis, on the Tigris River. The Babylonian forces were crushed and rendered incapable —

---

1. Cf. the *Nabonidus Chronicle,* iii, reverse. Translated by A. Leo Oppenheim in *Ancient Near Eastern Texts* (J. Prichard, ed.), p. 306.

psychologically as well as militarily — for further resistance. Babylon itself fell in October, 539. Belshazzar was killed and Nabonidus, who had fled, was subsequently imprisoned.

The impregnable walls of Babylon were of no help to Nabonidus, for his capital city surrendered without a fight. Gobryas, the governor of Gutium, is probably to be identified with the Biblical "Darius the Mede" who led the Persian troops into Babylon (Dan. 5:30).

When Cyrus personally entered Babylon he was welcomed by the populace. He proclaimed peace to everyone in the city. The temples functioned as usual and care was taken to make the transition to Persian rule as painless as possible. Gobryas was made satrap of the new province of Babirush (i.e., Babylon) and many of the former officials of government were kept at their posts. A citizen of Babylon would have been unaware of the fact that a new era of history had begun.

One aspect of the new policy of Cyrus had important bearings on subsequent Biblical history. Nabonidus had antagonized the Babylonian priesthood by bringing into the city the gods of other regions. Cyrus made it a point to return these captive gods, with due reverence, to their former shrines. This directly affected the Jews for, although there were no images of their God in Babylon, vessels from His Temple in Jerusalem had been taken by Nebuchadnezzar.

During the first year of his reign in Babylon, Cyrus issued a decree authorizing the rebuilding of the Jerusalem Temple and the restoration of the gold and silver vessels which were in Babylon. The expense of the project was to be met from the royal treasury (Ezra 6:3-5). To accomplish this it was necessary to permit such Jews as wished to do so, to return to their ancestral homeland and rebuild the city of Jerusalem. There was no thought that Jews would be required to leave Babylon, or other parts of the Persian Empire. As a matter of fact only a small remnant had any desire to return. It was that remnant, however, which made possible subsequent Palestinian Jewish history.

The return of the sacred vessels and the leadership of the band of Jews who chose to return to Jerusalem was entrusted to a Jewish noble, or "prince of Judah" named Shesh-bazzar. The name appears as Sanabassar in I Esdras and Josephus and probably was the Babylonian name Sin-ab-usur. It is possible that Shenazzar (I Chron. 3:18), a son of Jehoiachin, is the same person as Shesh-bazzar, the "prince of Judah" (Ezra 1:8).

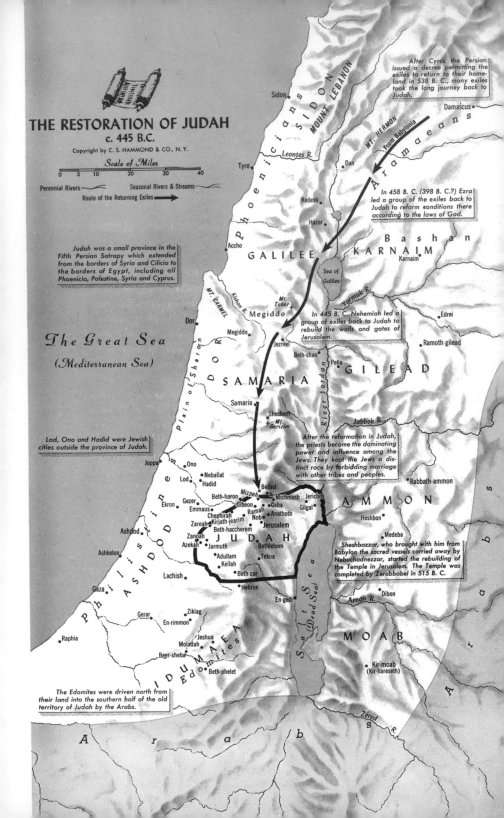

THE RESTORATION OF JUDAH
c. 445 B.C.

Copyright by C. S. HAMMOND & CO., N.Y.

Scale of Miles

0 5 10   20   30   40

Perennial Rivers ⌃⌃⌃⌃⌃⌃
Seasonal Rivers & Streams ⌃⌃⌃⌃⌃
Route of the Returning Exiles ➡

After Cyrus the Persian issued a decree permitting the exiles to return to their homeland in 538 B. C., many exiles took the long journey back to Judah.

In 458 B. C. (398 B. C.?) Ezra led a group of the exiles back to Judah to reform conditions there according to the laws of God.

Judah was a small province in the Fifth Persian Satrapy which extended from the borders of Syria and Cilicia to the borders of Egypt, including all Phoenicia, Palestine, Syria and Cyprus.

In 445 B. C. Nehemiah led a group of exiles back to Judah to rebuild the walls and gates of Jerusalem.

Lod, Ono and Hadid were Jewish cities outside the province of Judah.

After the reformation in Judah, the priests became the dominating power and influence among the Jews. They kept the Jews a distinct race by forbidding marriage with other tribes and peoples.

Sheshbazzar, who brought with him from Babylon the sacred vessels carried away by Nebuchadnezzar, started the rebuilding of the Temple in Jerusalem. The Temple was completed by Zerubbabel in 515 B. C.

The Edomites were driven north from their land into the southern half of the old territory of Judah by the Arabs.

The Great Sea
(Mediterranean Sea)

SIDON
Sidon
PHOENICIANS
MOUNT LEBANON
Leontes R.
Tyre
Damascus
MT. HERMON
From Babylonia
Aramaeans
Dan
Kedesh
Hazor
Accho
GALILEE
Bashan
KARNAIM
Karnaim
Sea of Galilee
MT. CARMEL
Kishon R.
Mt. Tabor
Megiddo
Megiddo
Yarmuk R.
Dor
DOR
Jezreel
Beth-shan
Pella
GILEAD
Edrei
Ramoth-gilead
Plain of Sharon
SAMARIA
Samaria
Shechem
Mt. Gerizim
Jabbok R.
River Jordan
Joppa
Ono
Neballat
Lod
Hadid
Bethel
Ai Michmash
Jericho
Gilgal
AMMON
Rabbath-ammon
Heshbon
Ekron
Gezer
Emmaus
Beth-horon
Gibeon
Geba
Anathoth
Chephirah
Ramah
Nob
Kirjath-jearim
Jerusalem
Zareah
Beth-haccherem
Medeba
Zanoah
Azekah
JUDAH
Bethlehem
Ashdod
Jarmuth
Adullam
Tekoa
Keilah
ASHDOD
PHILISTINE
Ashkelon
Beth-zur
Gaza
Lachish
Hebron
Dibon
Salt Sea (Dead Sea)
En-gedi
Arnon R.
Gerar
Ziklag
MOAB
En-rimmon
Raphia
Jeshua
Molatah
Beer-sheba
IDUMAEA
Edomites
Beth-phelet
Kir-moab
(Kir-hareseth)
Zered R.
Arabs
Arabia

The relationship between Shesh-bazzar and Zerubbabel is enigmatic. Many scholars suggest that they are different names for the same individual. In Ezra 5:14, however, Shesh-bazzar is mentioned as though he were dead ("one whose name was Shesh-bazzar") although Zerubbabel was clearly alive at the time. It may be that Shesh-bazzar died soon after the return to Jerusalem and Zerubbabel became his successor. Zerubbabel, a name meaning "seed of Babylon," i.e., "begotten in Babylon," was the son of Shealtiel (Ezra 3:2), hence the grandson of Jehoiachin (I Chron. 3:17). If Shesh-bazzar was a son of Jehoiachin, then he was uncle to Zerubbabel.

The first group of Jews to trek back to their homeland numbered close to 50,000. There were 42,360 free citizens, 7,337 slaves, and 200 Temple singers (Ezra 2:64-65). It was doubtless an enthusiastic group that journeyed back to Jerusalem a half century after its destruction by Nebuchadnezzar's army. These pilgrims would eagerly anticipate the fulfillment of prophecies of Jeremiah and Ezekiel, and see, in the return to Judah, a new beginning for their people.

The first responsibility of the returnees was the erection of a sanctuary and the renewal of the Levitical worship which had been held in abeyance since the destruction of the first Temple. An altar was first erected, and daily burnt offerings were made under the direction of Jeshua (or Joshua), the High Priest. Jeshua was the grandson of Seraiah who had served as the last High Priest before the destruction of the Temple in 587 B.C.

However enthusiastic the first group of pilgrims returning to Zion may have been, there is no question that they soon found reason for discouragement. The country was desolate, and squatters from among the Edomites, Moabites, Ammonites, Philistines, and Samaritans had profited by the absence of the Jews by occupying the Judaean countryside. The Samaritans, in particular, were openly hostile.

Shortly after the commencement of corporate life around the rebuilt altar, the Jews had an important decision to make. A group of Samaritans approached Zerubbabel with the suggestion, "Let us build with you; for we worship your God as you do, and we have been sacrificing to him ever since the days of Esarhaddon king of Syria who brought us here" (Ezra 4:2). The leaders of Israel were unwilling to form such a co-operative venture. Samaritan worship was syncretistic in the eyes of the Jews. The Samaritans had merely added the worship of Yahweh, the God of Israel, to the gods they had brought with them when they entered the land (II Kings 17:29-34). The Jewish leaders declined the Samaritan offer of assistance, noting that Cyrus had given to *them* the responsibility for rebuilding the Temple (Ezra 4:3). The Exile had been a bitter experience, and pious Jews were persuaded that the idolatry of their fathers had brought it about. They were determined that the post-exilic nation would be uncorrupted by heathen practices.

As might be expected, the Samaritans were hostile following this rebuff. They used every means at their command to frustrate the Jews in their efforts to build the Temple, and were successful in delaying the completion of the work until the reign of Darius (Ezra 4:5).

Shortly after Cyrus conquered Babylon he installed his son, Cambyses, as governor of Babirush (Babylonia), thus preparing him for the day when he would succeed his father to the throne of the Empire. Cyrus was killed during a military campaign in 528 B.C. and Cambyses took the throne. Under Cambyses, Egypt was incorporated into the Persian Empire and Egyptian autonomy came to an end. The Jews would look with favor on such a move for the Persians had treated them well. Cyrus may have seen the wisdom of having a friendly state on the border of Egypt at the time he issued his decree permitting Jews to return to their homeland. The Nabataean Arabs supplied the troops of Cambyses with water in the desert regions which separate Judah from Egypt.

In 522 B.C. Cambyses died. He was on his way home from Egypt when he received word that a usurper had seized the throne and was recognized as king by the eastern provinces of the Empire. It is thought that Cambyses took his own life, but the circumstances are obscure. An officer of Cambyses, himself of royal blood, claimed the throne as Cambyses' successor, marched against Gaumata, the usurper, and executed him. A period of rebellion ensued, and all parts of the Empire were affected. For two years Darius had to quell opposition in Babylon, Asia Minor, Egypt, and his eastern provinces — Media, Elam, Parsa, and Iran.

Where was Judah at this time? Its Temple had not been completed, but it is certain that the international upheavals spurred the people on to renewed activity. Could the Messianic Age, long hoped for, be at hand? Judah was but a part of the friendly Persian Empire, but she did have hopes of a day when a Davidic king would rule from a rebuilt Jerusalem.

Such hopes were particularly stressed by the prophets Haggai and Zechariah. Through their exhortations the leaders determined to take up the task of building the Temple which had been neglected because the people felt the time inopportune (Hag. 1:2; Ezra 5:1-2). The prophets pleaded for a purified Israel, separate from all heathen associations (cf. Hag. 2:10-14). To a purified nation, the "Branch" of David's line would appear (Zech. 3:8).

To what extent could such hopes be considered treason in the Persian court? The Samaritans would surely twist them to imply a plot on the part of the Jews to start an insurrection. Tattenai, the satrap of Abar-nahara, the satrapy which included Palestine and Syria, felt called upon to investigate the building operations of the Jews (Ezra 5:3-5). The Jews told him of the decree of Cyrus, and Tattenai sent to the Persian court to check their claims. In the state archives at Ecbatana, Darius found the decree of Cyrus, whereupon he ordered Tattenai to expedite the work of the Jews and meet the cost of their work from the royal treasury (Ezra 6:6-12).

The work went forward until March, 515 B.C., when the Second Temple was dedicated amid scenes of great rejoicing (Ezra 6:13-18). The new Temple was small in comparison with that built by Solomon. Israel was no longer a prosperous, sovereign state with kings who received tribute from distant lands. Instead it was a part of the Persian Empire, paying tribute to gentile kings. Nevertheless the Second Temple was to become a rallying point for post-exilic Israel.

Zerubbabel quietly, if not mysteriously, passes from the scene. Some think the Persians feared his political goals and removed him as a potential rebel. We do know that the Persians chose to rule the Jews through their High Priests — Jeshua and his successors. Perhaps they heard of the Messianic hopes of the Jews and felt that it would be safer to work through the priests than through secular princes who traced their lineage to David.

17

EZRA THE SCRIBE

Among the Biblical characters of the post-exilic period none assumes a greater historical importance than Ezra. There has been considerable disagreement concerning the date of Ezra, for some very able scholars feel that our texts have been dislocated and that Nehemiah should be placed before Ezra.[1] The traditional order, maintained in the Massoretic Text of Scripture, fits in well with our knowledge of the post-exilic age and may be adhered to until convincing evidence to the contrary is produced.

Over fifty years pass in silence between the dedication of the Second Temple (515 B.C.) and the arrival of Ezra in Palestine in the seventh year of Artaxerxes (457 B.C.). Although successful in building the Temple, the Palestinian Jews were certainly not a prosperous group during this period. Their city had no walls and it was open to attack from their numerous enemies. The people had become dispirited. Earlier resolves to live lives of separation from their neighbors had been quietly forgotten and mixed marriage was common.

Back in Babylon and in other parts of the Persian Empire there were numerous Jews who still looked with fond associations to Jerusalem as the center of their religious life and their spiritual hopes. Such a man was Ezra, a pious Levite who had devoted his life to the study of God's Law. As a lover of Zion, Ezra appealed to Artaxerxes for help in making it possible for a fresh company of exiles to return to the land of their fathers. The king granted his request (Ezra 7:11-26) and authorized Ezra to assemble such Jews as would volunteer to join him on the journey to Palestine. Ezra was authorized to take with him offerings for the Jerusalem Temple sent both by Artaxerxes and

---

1. H. H. Rowley, "The Chronological Order of Ezra and Nehemiah," in *The Servant of the Lord and other Essays on the Old Testament*, pp. 131-159.

by the Jewish community. Ezra was instructed to use it to purchase sacrificial animals. The remainder could be spent as Ezra
and his brethren saw fit (Ezra 7:17-18). Authority was also given
to draw upon the royal treasury of the province of Syria if necessary (Ezra 7:20). Ezra was further authorized to appoint magis-
trates and judges and to teach the Law of God and the king to
any who might not be familiar with it. The Law was to be
rigorously enforced by imprisonment, confiscation of property,
banishment, or even death (Ezra 7:26). Empowered in this way,
Ezra was not merely a pious pilgrim but a representative of the
Persian government with power to act. The provincial rulers
were told, "Whatever Ezra the priest, the scribe of the Law of the
God of heaven, requires of you, be it done with all diligence"
(Ezra 7:21).

In all, about eighteen hundred men and their families responded to Ezra's appeal (Ezra 8:1-14). As the group gathered
at Ahava, Ezra noted that there were no priests in the company.
A special appeal was made and thirty-eight priests and two
hundred and twenty Temple servants joined the party (Ezra
8:15-20). Artaxerxes in his decree had exempted priests and
Temple servants from the Persian tax. Their reluctance to come
may indicate that they were comfortably settled in Persia and
felt no emotional ties with Jerusalem.

Having assured Artaxerxes of his confidence in divine protection, Ezra did not feel justified in requesting the usual military
escort (Ezra 8:22). The group fasted and prayed (Ezra 8:23)
before starting out on a journey of four months. No details are
given concerning the journey itself, but we know that Erza entrusted the silver, the gold, and the vessels which were to be
brought to the Jerusalem Temple into the hands of the priests
and Levites (Ezra 8:24-30).

As a delegated representative of the Persian Crown in Jerusalem Ezra bore the title, "Scribe of the law of the God of
heaven" (Ezra 7:12). In modern language we might designate
him, "Minister of State for Jewish Affairs."[2] The Persians were
tolerant of the many religions in their Empire, but they did wish
them to be regularized under responsible authority. Ezra, armed
with his official rescript, was responsible for Jewish affairs in the
province of Abar-nahara, i.e., Syria and Palestine (Ezra 7:25).

Shortly after their arrival in Jerusalem, Ezra and his company
brought their treasures to the Temple and offered special sac-

---

2. Cf. John Bright, *A History of Israel*, p. 370.

rifices on the altar in the Temple court. They could testify that,
". . . the hand of our God was upon us, and he delivered us from
the hand of the enemy and from ambushes by the way" (Ezra
8:31).

Ezra did not find the populace enthusiastic about the measures
which were close to his heart. Some of the people had grown
prosperous (Hag. 1:4), but spirituality was largely missing.
Many of the Jews, including priests and Levites, had taken
foreign wives (Ezra 9:1). Marriage, to Ezra, was not simply a
matter of social arrangement, but one which involved obedience
to the Law of God. Of the Gentile nations God had said, "You
shall not make marriages with them, giving your daughters to
their sons or taking their daughters for your sons" (Deut. 7:3).
Intermarriage, as in the case of Solomon (I Kings 11:1-8), was
a prelude to idolatry — the sin which had brought on the Babylonian Exile. Moved to contrition as he associated himself with
his sinning compatriots, Ezra poured out his soul to God in confession and penitence (Ezra 9:6-15).

As the people gathered around Ezra, one of their number,
Shecaniah, suggested that they all put away their foreign wives
and their children (Ezra 10:2-3). Ezra then proposed that all
Israel, led by the priests and Levites, vow to do as Shecaniah had
suggested (Ezra 10:5). A decree was issued that all the people
should assemble at Jerusalem within three days under penalty
of confiscation of goods and excommunication (Ezra 10:7-8).
When the people assembled they found that the task was too
great to accomplish in the open square during a rain storm
(Ezra 10:9-15). A divorce court was established (Ezra 10:16-17)
and arrangements were made for the Jewish men to put away
their foreign wives and children (Ezra 10:44).

Ezra's attitude in the matter of the foreign women was governed by his zeal for purity of Jewish life and faith. He was willing to sacrifice anything (and any one) that endangered that
purity. His edict was certainly resented by many Jews and there
can be no doubt that it stirred up the non-Jewish population in
hostility against their Jewish neighbors.

Ezra had brought with him from Babylon "the Book of the
Law of Moses" (Neh. 8:1) which he publicly read from a wooden
pulpit (Neh. 8:4). Along with the reading there was an explanation (Neh. 8:8), probably in the Aramaic language which had
become the popular language of the Jews during the time of
their exile. When the people learned that it was the time of the
Feast of Tabernacles which, through ignorance, they were not

observing, they built booths for themselves and observed the ancient feast (Neh. 8:14-18).

The feast was followed by a solemn fast during which the Jews separated themselves from all foreigners and confessed their sin (Neh. 9:2). Again the Law was read (Ezra 9:4) and Ezra uttered a remarkable prayer in which he traced the mercies of God to Israel and deplored his people's unfaithfulness (Ezra 9:6-37). The princes, Levites, and priests solemnly covenanted before all the people to be faithful to God's Law (Neh. 9:38).

What was this Law that Ezra brought to Jerusalem? It was certainly not a new law, for it professed to go back to the days of Joshua (Neh. 8:17). It is termed "the Law of Moses" and was studied by the Jews of Babylon as the revelation of God's will which had been given to Moses at Mount Sinai. Whether Ezra had the completed Pentateuch, or some portion of it, we cannot say. We do know that the Babylonian Jews became diligent students of the Law during the period of the Exile.

This Law was received by the Palestinian Jewish community in solemn covenant before their God (Neh. 10). Although they lacked political independence, they became a religious community, subject to a religious Law. This was to mark the future of Judaism. Jews might exist under a variety of governments, but all could cherish the Law. They might be removed geographically from the Temple, or the Temple might be destroyed (as it was by the armies of Titus, A.D. 70), but the Law would still be theirs to cherish and obey. Legends were to develop around the person of Ezra, but his relationship to Israel as a second lawgiver, makes them unnecessary. His place in Jewish history is secure. Later generations said, "When the Law had been forgotten in Israel, Ezra came up from Babylon and established it."[3] A second century Jewish scholar, Rabbi Jose of Palestine gave him the highest compliment: "Ezra was worthy of having the Law given through him to Israel, had not Moses preceded him."[4]

---

3. Quoted in G. F. Moore, *Judaism*, I, p. 7
4. Quoted in Harry M. Orlinsky, *Ancient Israel*, p. 136.

18

NEHEMIAH THE BUILDER

A Persian Jew named Nehemiah had risen to the post of cup-bearer[1] to Artaxerxes Longimanus (465-424 B.C.). This was a position of honor[2] for it involved an intimate relationship with the king. One of the responsibilities of the cupbearer was to taste the wine to see that it was not poisoned. He thus became the king's confidant.

When his brother Hanani and others from Judah came to visit Nehemiah at the Persian court, they told him of the difficulties of the Jews in Palestine (Neh. 1:1-3). Jerusalem had no walls to protect it from its many enemies. Although reckoned as the Holy City because the Temple of the Lord had been built there, few people dared live among its ruins.

Nehemiah was filled with grief at the report of the suffering of his brethren in Palestine. He prayed for guidance and sought an opportunity to present his burden to the king. Four months went by before Nehemiah could present his request. Then Artaxerxes, noticing the sadness of his cupbearer, asked Nehemiah to explain his problem (Neh. 2:1-3).

When Nehemiah told the king of his burden for Jerusalem, Artaxerxes readily granted him a leave of absence to visit the city and do the work that was on his heart. The length of the leave was agreed upon (Neh. 2:6) and Artaxerxes issued a royal re-script authorizing the building of the walls of Jerusalem. Letters were sent to the governors of the provinces west of the Euphrates and to Asaph, the keeper of the royal forest directing that Nehemiah be provided with the materials he would need for the gates of the citadel, for the wall of the city, and for the Temple itself

---

1. For the office of cupbearer, cf. Xenophon, *Cyropaedia*, i. 3, 4. Nehemiah was probably an eunuch. This would account for the fact that he had access to the king when the queen also was present (cf. Neh. 2:6).
2. Cf. Herodotus, *Histories*, iii, 34.

(Neh. 2:7-8). Nehemiah was appointed governor of Judah (Neh. 5:14), thus making it a province separate from Samaria. This was to be one factor in the rivalry that developed between Sanballat, governor of Samaria, and Nehemiah.

The generosity of Artaxerxes was not without political implications and possible benefit to Persia. Egypt had been perennially restive, and Persia wanted her Palestinian provinces which bordered Egypt to be in friendly, loyal hands. The Jews, moreover, had smarted under Samaritan officialdom and were generally demoralized. If successful in his mission, Nehemiah could help both his own people and the king whom he served.

After making necessary preparations, Nehemiah and a group of companions made the long journey from Susa to Jerusalem. His first concern was for the building of the walls of the city. In the company of a few associates he inspected the ruined walls by night (Neh. 2:12-15). Again his heart was heavy. A city without walls was not really a city at all. The ruined walls were a reproach both to Judah and to Judah's God (Neh. 2:17).

After inspecting the ruins, Nehemiah sought out the leaders of the Jerusalem community — the priests and nobles (Neh. 2:16-17) — and explained his mission. He told them of the way in which God had prospered his efforts and the co-operation which had been promised by Artaxerxes (Neh. 2:18). The response of the leaders of Jerusalem was gratifying. They caught something of Nehemiah's enthusiasm and said "Let us rise up and build" (Neh. 2:18).

Initial plans had no sooner been made when serious opposition developed. It found its focal point in three non-Jews, although important elements in Jerusalem were sympathetic with their plans. Sanballat, governor of Samaria, is identified as "the Horonite" (Neh. 2:19). He was probably a native of Beth-horon in Samaria. His companions are identified as Tobiah, an Ammonite slave, and Geshem, probably the chief of a tribe in northwestern Arabia. These men mocked the Jews for their efforts to rebuild the walls of Jerusalem and insinuated that this was an act of rebellion against Persia (Neh. 2:19-20).

Nehemiah pressed on with his plans. The people responded to his appeal for help and soon labor battalions were assigned to the various sections into which the wall had been divided. Workers came from outside villages — Jericho, Gibeon, Mizpah, Beth-haccherem, Zanoah, Beth-zur, Keilah, and Tekoa. Priests, Levites, goldsmiths, and merchants all labored together (Neh. 3).

Sanballat and his allies, seeing that mockery did not deter Nehemiah from his building program, determined to take more positive action. The wall had reached half its desired height (Neh. 4:6) and Sanballat determined to send guerilla bands against Jerusalem. Arabians, Ammonites, and Ashdodites (Neh. 4:7) began to harass the Jews who were working on the wall. They planned a sneak attack, but Nehemiah was ready for them (Neh. 4:11). He stationed armed men to guard the unprotected places in the wall (Neh. 4:13). When the enemy learned that the Jews were armed, they abandoned their plan to make a frontal attack (Neh. 4:15), but sought other means to hinder Nehemiah from accomplishing his goals.

From this time on the workmen were armed: "Each of the builders had his sword girded at his side while he built" (Neh. 4:18). A trumpeter stood beside Nehemiah ready to give warning in the event of attack. The people whose homes were outside the city were not permitted to leave Jerusalem. The enemy was in the outlying territory and the city could not be left without defenders. Neither Nehemiah nor his people removed their clothes at night. They slept with weapons at their side, ready to respond at the sound of the trumpet (Neh. 4:22-23). There is no record of an actual battle. The Samaritans and their allies did not make an open attack, but they posed a constant threat and worked serious hardships on the Jews.

Although able to stand up under pressures from without, Nehemiah faced the collapse of his cause as a result of internal problems. The people working on the walls had no source of income. Many had left homes and farms, only to have them looted and plundered by the enemy. People had to mortgage fields, vineyards, and houses to provide food and to pay their taxes (Neh. 5:3-4). Some had pledged their children for debt, and they were sold into slavery (Neh. 5:5). Isaac Mendelsohn notes, "Nehemiah 5:1-5 proves that in Palestine loans were obtained, as in Assyria, on security. Houses, fields, vineyards, olive groves, and children were pledged, and if the debts were not repaid, the creditors would retain the land as their property and the children as slaves."[3]

Nehemiah was angered at this report of the way in which the wealthy class had taken advantage of the poor during a time of national crisis (Neh. 5:6). He summoned the offenders to a public meeting, during which he reviewed his own financial rec-

---

3. *Legal Aspects of Slavery in Babylonia, Assyria and Palestine*, p. 19.

ord (Neh. 5:14-19). Nehemiah had refused to accept the allowances to which he was entitled as governor and had actually supported one hundred and fifty Jews at his own expense. The
nobles and officials who had exploited the poor responded to
Nehemiah's plea and vowed to restore that which they had taken
(Neh. 5:12).

Having failed in other ways, Nehemiah's enemies attempted
to defeat him by intrigue. Four times they invited him to confer
with them in the valley of Ono in Benjamin, but he insisted that
he could not leave the great work in which he was engaged
(Neh. 6:1-4). A fifth messenger came with an open letter from
Sanballat accusing Nehemiah of a conspiracy to rebel against
Persia and establish himself as king in Judah (Neh. 6:5-7). Nehemiah refused so much as to discuss the charge, bluntly stating
that they were the fabrication of Sanballat's evil mind (Neh.
6:8). Sanballat and Tobiah went so far as to hire prophets to in-
duce Nehemiah to lock himself in the Temple to avoid assassina-
tion. Nehemiah saw through this plot and refused to go (Neh.
6:10-13). It is a sad commentary on the religious life of the
times that men who considered themselves prophets could sell
their services to Judah's enemies.

Undisturbed by the many devices fashioned to deflect him
from his goal, Nehemiah pressed on toward the completion of
his work. In less than two months (Neh. 6:15) the wall was completed. Josephus tells us that it was further strengthened with
battlements and gates over an additional two years and four
months.[4] Nehemiah appointed his brother Hanani and a man
named Hananiah, the governor of the castle, to assume responsibility for the welfare of Jerusalem. He charged them to keep the
city gates closed until the sun was well up in the heavens, and to
keep a guard posted (Neh. 7:2-3).

The inhabitants of Jerusalem were few, for houses were still in
ruins. It was necessary to encourage people to settle within the
city, because life was more pleasant in other parts of Judah.
Those who volunteered to live in Jerusalem were highly regarded. They had to be augmented by a forced draft which brought
one-tenth of the country people into the Holy City (Neh. 11:1).

The completion of the walls was an occasion of celebration and
spiritual dedication. After ceremonies of purification (Neh.
12:30), two processions were formed to move around the walls in
opposite directions. Ezra was at the head of one company, and

---

4. *Antiquities,* XI, v, 8.

Nehemiah of the other. They met near the Temple area where
the people gave expression to their joy and offered appropriate
sacrifices (Neh. 12:31-43).

With the rebuilding of the walls and adequate provision made
for the observance of the sacrifices and holy days prescribed in
the Mosaic Law (Neh. 12:27-30), Nehemiah was free to end his
leave of absence and return to the Persian court (Neh. 13:6).
We can imagine the enthusiasm and the gratitude with which he
greeted Artaxerxes at Susa. The problems in Judah were not
over, however. Within a short time — perhaps from one to three
years — Nehemiah was granted a second leave of absence to return to Jerusalem.

During Nehemiah's absence at the Persian court, the situation
in Jerusalem had deteriorated. Although freed from the threat
of enemies from without, the Jews themselves grew careless and
internal dissention and infidelity brought on a new crisis. The
wine presses were in operation on the sabbath day, and Tyrian
merchants brought their fish and other merchandise into Jerusalem contrary to the Sabbath law (Neh. 13:15-16). The perennial
problem of intermarriage came to the fore again during the absence of Nehemiah (Neh. 13:23). Israelite men had married
women from Ashdod, Ammon, and Moab. The effect was evident
even in the speech of the people, for the language of these wives
was spoken by their children in the very streets of Jerusalem (Neh.
13:24). A grandson of Eliashib, the high priest, married a daughter of Nehemiah's inveterate enemy, Sanballat (Neh. 13:28).

The religious life of the people had also fallen into decay.
Eliashib befriended Nehemiah's enemy Tobiah, the Ammonite,
and housed him in one of the Temple chambers (Neh. 13:4-5).
The Levites were not given their allowances with the result that
they had to find other work to do (Neh. 13:10). Many returned
to their fields and earned their living as farmers.

When Nehemiah heard of these things he was understandably
disturbed. He returned to Jerusalem and, with characteristic
vigor, determined to set things right. Tobiah's belongings were
cast out of the Temple and it was restored to its sacred use (Neh.
13:8-9). The fiscal policy of the Temple was reorganized and
tithes of corn, wine, and oil were collected so that provision could
be made for the Levites to give their time to their Temple min-
istrations (Neh. 13:11-13). Nehemiah appealed to the leaders of
Jerusalem to close the city gates on the Sabbath Day (Neh.
13:17-18). The command for strict Sabbath observance was given
and, when some merchants attempted to circumvent the law by

selling their wares outside the city wall, Nehemiah threatened to forcibly remove them (Neh. 13:20-21).

The problem of intermarriage was a vexing one. Nehemiah asked the Jews to swear that they would not permit their children to marry into the families of neighboring peoples. He reminded them that even godly Solomon was led astray by his foreign wives (Neh. 13:25-27). Eliashib's grandson, who had married the daughter of Sanballet, was a notorious offender and Nehemiah banished him from Jerusalem (Neh. 13:28).

An important sequel to this episode is recorded by Josephus,[5] who states that Manasseh (the grandson of Eliashib) married Sanballat's daughter, Nicaso. When Nehemiah gave him the choice between abdicating his priestly office or divorcing his wife, Manasseh took the problem to his father-in-law. Sanballat, we are told, offered to make Manasseh the High Priest in Samaria and promised to build for him a temple on Mount Gerizim as soon as the permission of the Persian king (Darius, in Josephus' account) could be secured. He further promised to make Manasseh his successor as governor of Samaria.

Josephus was evidently following Samaritan sources in his account of the building of the temple on Mount Gerizim. He states that Sanballat offered his troops to Alexander (!) upon his entrance into Palestine following the battle at Issus, and gained as a boon the permission to build the temple on Mount Gerizim. Josephus tells us that many priests and Levites went to Samaria with Manasseh and that they were given lands in Samaria by Sanballat.

The chief objection to the record as given by Josephus is the chronological discrepancy of placing Sanballat in the era of Alexander the Great — a century later than the time of Nehemiah. This misplacement of the episode need not argue against its essential historicity, however. James A. Montgomery notes:

> The age of the Conqueror is the one bright point in the reminiscences of the ancient world, and was a shining mark for the art of legend-manufacture. Just as the Jews had their legend concerning Alexander's favor to Jerusalem, so the Samaritans told their fables concerning his connection with their sect and temple; probably in this point Josephus was depending upon some Samaritan tradition, which he, or rather the legend-cycle which he followed, brought into connection with the history of Sanballat.[6]

It is clear from the Biblical picture of Nehemiah that his leadership was not unchallenged. An important party in Jerusalem was sympathetic with Sanballat. During the absence of Nehemiah

---

5. *Antiquities,* XI, vii. 2; viii. 2.
6. *The Samaritans,* p. 69.

they came to positions of prominence, but with his return they were put on the defensive. With the expulsion of Manasseh, their power was broken, the schism became permanent, and Jew and Samaritan went their separate ways.

Nehemiah is best remembered for his work on the rebuilding of the walls of Jerusalem. Sirach says of him, "... he raised for us the walls that had fallen, and set up the gates and bars and rebuilt our ruined houses" (Sir. 49:13). Josephus echoes, "He was a man of good and righteous character, and very ambitious to make his own nation happy; and he hath left the walls of Jerusalem as an eternal monument of himself."[7]

---

7. *Antiquities,* **XI**, v. 8.

19

ESTHER AND THE PERSIAN COURT

The focus of attention in the books of Ezra and Nehemiah is upon the faithful remnant of Jews who returned to Palestine in the years following the decree of Cyrus. Jewish life continued in the East, since many who thought of themselves as loyal Jews, preferred to live in their adopted country.

The incidents described in the Biblical book of Esther indicate some of the trials and victories experienced by Jews who chose to remain in Babylon and Persia. We find ourselves in the court of Xerxes (486-465 B.C.), son and successor of Darius the Great. The king provided lavish entertainment for his nobles and, at the height of his party, sent for his queen, Vashti, and ordered her to make a lewd display of herself. When Vashti refused, the nobles suggested that Vashti be deposed lest her refusal to obey the king become an example to other wives who might not respect the word of their husbands.

It was in the third year of Xerxes (Biblical Ahasuerus) that Vashti was deposed, and four years were to pass before another queen would be chosen. These were difficult years for the Persian king who had determined to conquer Greece. In 480 B.C. Greece defeated the Persians in a naval encounter at Salamis, and the next year was one of further reverses for Persia at Plataea. Xerxes was far from achieving his goals on the field of battle.

When the king decided to find a wife to take the place of Vashti he sent to the many provinces of his Empire to secure young ladies from whom the choice might be made. We might term this an ancient beauty contest. The plan was suggested by the courtiers of Xerxes and approved by the king himself.

Among the young ladies brought to Susa (Biblical Shushan), the capital of Susiana and winter palace of the Persian kings, was a Jewess named Hadassah, or Esther, the cousin of a Jew of Susa named Mordecai. Mordecai was a faithful Jew who could trace

Air view of Susa (Biblical Shushan). Susa was the royal winter residence of Darius the Great, and served as one of three capitals of the Persian Empire. The excavated ruins show levels of occupation from about 4000 B.C. to A.D. 1200.

Courtesy, Oriental Institute

his ancestry back to Benjamin (Esther 2:5). The name of Mordecai appears in the Persian and Neo-Babylonian cuneiform literature. We know that a man named Mordecai (Marduka) was a high officer in the court of Susa during the early days of Xerxes' reign.[1] The German cuneiform scholar, Arthur Ungnad, asserts that this text which was discovered at Borsippa is our first and only extra-Biblical reference to the Mordecai of the Esther story. Mordecai bore a name which honored Marduk, the god of Babylon. The name was a common one, and Ungnad's identification need not be insisted on. We do know that a faithful Jew with that name was in Susa at the time.

The ancestors of Esther and Mordecai had been deported from Jerusalem with Jehoiachin in 597 B.C. (Esther 2:6). When Esther's parents died, her cousin, Mordecai, assumed responsibility for her. Conscious of her great beauty, Mordecai brought Esther to the court where she immediately captivated Xerxes. She may have been conscious of anti-Semitic feelings at court, for she did not reveal the fact that she was a Jewess. In the seventh year of his reign, amidst scenes of rejoicing, Xerxes married Esther (Esther 2:17-18).

Trouble came to a head for the Jews when Haman, termed "the Agagite" (after the Amalekite king defeated by Saul) was chosen as grand vizier to Xerxes (Esther 3:1). Mordecai, proud of his Jewish blood and conscious of ancient rivalries between Jews and Amalekites, refused to bow before Haman. Incensed by this lack of respect, Haman determined to have all of the Jews in Persia executed.

By casting a lot ("pur," from which the Jewish holiday Purim is named), Haman determined that the thirteenth day of Adar (February-March) was the most auspicious day for his pogram. He then told Xerxes of "a certain people" scattered throughout the Empire who refused to obey the king's laws. Haman was so anxious to destroy these "people" that he offered to pay to the royal treasury ten thousand silver talents (about eighteen million dollars), if the king would back his project. Xerxes placed his signet ring on Haman's hand and authorized him to proceed with his plans. Orders were dispatched to the provincial governors to destroy all of the Jews on the thirteenth of Adar, eleven months from the date of the edict.

---

1. Cf. A. Ungnad, "Keilinschriftliche Beitrage zum Buch Esra und Ester," *Zeitschrift für die Alttestamentliche Wissenschaft,* LVIII (1940-41) pp. 240-244.

Mordecai and the Jews mourned when they learned of the decree which had been devised to exterminate them. Esther, unaware of what had happened, sent for Mordecai, providing him
with a suitable robe so that he might visit the palace. Mordecai
refused to come, but sent Esther a copy of the decree, and urged
her to intervene on behalf of her people. She, in turn, replied
that she could not appear before the king unannounced. Such an
act might anger the king and cause him to kill her. Mordecai
warned Esther that the enforcement of the decree would bring
about her death in any event (Esther 4:13) and suggested that
she had "come to the kingdom for such a time as this" (Esther
4:14). With the heroic words, "If I perish, I perish" (Esther
4:16), Esther determined to go to the king.

When she entered the forbidden inner court, Esther was
graciously received by the king. Instead of stating her request she
invited Xerxes and his vizier, Haman to dinner (Esther 5:1-4).
When the wine was served at the end of the meal she invited
them to a second banquet the next day. Haman, overjoyed at the
deference paid him by the queen, was later annoyed as he passed
Mordecai (Esther 5:9). Determining to rid himself of this hated
Jew he erected a gallows over 83 feet high on which to hang his
imagined foe (Esther 5:14).

That night when Xerxes had difficulty sleeping he ordered the
royal chronicles read to him (Esther 6:1-3). When the account
of Mordecai's act in saving the king from a conspiracy on his life
(Esther 2:21-23) was reached, Xerxes insisted that some suitable
reward should be provided for his faithful courtier. Haman came
early to ask permission to hang Mordecai, but before he could
make known his request, the king asked him to suggest a means
of honoring a particularly faithful subject. Haman, thinking that
he was the one to be honored, suggested that the man be led
through the streets on horseback, attired in royal garments and
preceded by a herald proclaiming the meaning of the honor.
Crestfallen when he learned that Mordecai was the man to be
honored, Haman nevertheless carried out his own recommenda-
tion (Esther 6:4-11). Returning home he found his wife and
friends pessimistic about his contest with Mordecai. While they
were talking, the king's chamberlain came to take Haman to the
queen's banquet (Esther 6:12-14).

At the end of the meal, Esther, at the king's request, presented
her petition (Esther 7:3-4). She asked that she and her people
be spared from the destruction which had been determined.
Wondering who had plotted such evil, Xerxes was told that it

was none other than his grand vizier, Haman. While the king, in great agitation, walked in the garden, Haman approached Esther to plead for his life. Returning, however, the king saw Haman with the queen and suspected him of assaulting her. Xerxes ordered that Haman be executed on the gallows that had been built for Mordecai (Esther 7:5-10).

Unable to revoke the edict of Haman, the king authorized Mordecai, his new grand vizier, to issue a decree permitting the Jews to massacre and despoil all who would attack them on the fateful thirteenth of Adar (Esther 8:8-14). The Jews rejoiced at this new decree and many of their neighbors professed to become Jews to avoid the retribution which they feared the Jews would take upon their enemies (Esther 8:16-17).[2]

On the thirteenth of Adar the two decrees went into effect. Because of the influence of Mordecai, the provincial rulers sided with the Jews in their conflict with their enemies. In Susa the Jews slew five hundred men in addition to the ten sons of Haman (Esther 9:1-11). The king acceded to Esther's request that the Jews be granted a second day to take vengeance on their enemies, and on the fourteenth of Adar they slew three hundred more (Esther 9:13-16). In the provinces the Jews had slain 75,000 of their enemies on the thirteenth of Adar, and celebrated a joyous festival on the fourteenth (Esther 9:16-17). The Septuagint gives the number killed as 15,000. In Susa the Jews celebrated their victory on the fifteenth of Adar. Mordecai and Esther wrote letters instructing the Jews to celebrate Purim both on the fourteenth and fifteenth of Adar by "feasting and gladness, sending portions (of food) one to another, and gifts to the poor."

Among the unusual characteristics of the Book of Esther is the total absence of the word "God." Although we do read of fasting, there is no mention of prayer. Mordecai and Esther both appear as godly Jews, however. In the dire need which faced them following Haman's decree, Mordecai suggested that if Esther did not go to the king deliverance might come "from another place" (Esther 4:14), an expression which implies the intervention of God. Although far from the land of Palestine, the Persian Jews knew that their God ever stood "within the shadows keeping watch above His own."

---

2. Cyrus Gordon interprets this as an example of the doctrine of *kitman* or dissimulation which permits one to deny his religion and pose as a member of another religion to avoid danger. He points out that Esther hid her Jewish affiliation (Esther 2:10) before the Iranian gentiles pretended to be Jews (Esther 8:17). Cf. Cyrus H. Gordon, *The World of the Old Testament*, pp. 283-284.

20

THE EMERGENCE OF JUDAISM

During the years of exile Israel became a religious community which was not related to any political entity or cultic center. This fact made changes in her thinking and her political institutions which have continued to the present. Although some Jews would later return to Jerusalem, the majority would continue to live at a distance from the Holy Land. Their ties would be cultural and religious, but not political.

The term "Israel" is frequently used to describe the earlier period of Jewish life, when the tribes dwelt in proximity to one another and religious life was conveniently centered in one central sanctuary. As a political unit, Israel was a world power in the days of David and Solomon, and even after the division of the kingdom she remained a political force to be reckoned with. After the Exile, Judah remained a subject state which, except for the Maccabean interlude, was dependent upon the great powers among whom she lived — Persia, Macedonia, the Ptolemies of Egypt, the Syrian Seleucids, and Rome. Her people lived not only in Palestine, but also in Egypt, Persia, Babylon, Syria, Asia Minor, Greece, and Rome. These Jews might visit Jerusalem at the great religious festivals (cf. Acts 2:8-11), but they had found their livelihood in a wider world and made some adaptations to a wider culture.

Exilic and post-exilic Judaism was the heir to the Law and the prophetic writings of pre-exilic Israel. The Exile itself had underscored the need of faithfulness to Israel's God. Idolatry had been the besetting sin of the pre-exilic period, and those who had suffered the loss of home and Temple could be expected to turn in horror from the sins which brought on the Exile.

The Israeli scholar, Yehezkel Kaufmann, has summarized the effect of the Exile upon the Jewish tendency toward idolatry:

Vestiges of an ancient fetishistic idolatry reinforced by foreign influences, continued to exist among the people down to the fall of Judah. It was the catastrophe of the Fall that aroused in the people a spirit of remorse. The pious viewed the sin of idolatry as the crucial national sin. The prophets had predicted doom for the worship of gods of wood and stone. God-fearing kings such as Asa, Jehoshaphat, Hezekiah, and Josiah had destroyed idolatrous cults, but had been unable to root out idolatry entirely. The Fall worked a revolution. The nation accepted the verdict that God's wrath had poured down upon them for the sin of idolatry, and they drew the ultimate conclusion from their monotheistic faith: all traces of idol-worship must be extirpated. It was thus in the realm of the cult that the final victory of monotheism in Israel took place. Henceforth Israel was a nation jealous for its Jealous God.[1]

The rejection of idolatry had, as its positive side, a deepening appreciation of Israel's historic monotheistic faith as enunciated in the body of sacred writings known as the Torah, or Law. Torah must not be thought of as law in the restricted sense of rules for conduct. The Torah contains such, of course, but it includes a great deal more. The Hebrew Torah is our Pentateuch — the first five books of the Bible. Parts of Exodus, Leviticus, and Deuteronomy give us codified law, but much of the Torah instructs us by example. Biographies of godly men — Abraham, Joseph, Noah, Moses — and a host of others, provide instruction. The evil deeds of men so realistically described, provide instruction also. Bad examples as well as good examples are necessary if we are to understand life in its totality. The evil must be shunned, and the good imitated, but both are illustrated and described in the Torah of Israel.

Kaufmann observes the need for Torah in exilic Judaism: "With land, temple, and king gone, only one contact with the holy was left, the divine word."[2] There were no Jewish altars in Babylon. The Jews shrank even from singing the songs of Zion in the land of exile (Psalm 137:4). The Scriptures — the Bible of ancient Israel — filled the vacuum produced by the crisis of Exile.

Not only the Law, but pre-exilic prophetic writings were studied by faithful Jews in Babylon. Daniel tells us that it was his study of the prophecies of Jeremiah that caused him to humble himself before God in anticipation of the day when the enforced exile would come to an end (Dan. 9:1-19). In contemplating the time when a new Temple would be built in Jerusalem, the priests and their descendants concerned themselves with the minutia of the Levitical laws. Those whose hearts were still in Zion occupied themselves with the Scriptures. There

---

1. "The Biblical Age," in *Great Ages and Ideas of the Jewish People,* p. 79.
2. *The Religion of Israel,* p. 448.

they learned both the reason for the Exile and the manner of life which the people of God should live both in the land of their captivity and, at a later time, in a restored Zion.

The synagogue, the characteristic institution of post-exilic Judaism, had its roots in the religious needs of those who could not attend the Temple worship to which they were accustomed. Orthodox Judaism permitted but one Sanctuary, that which had first been built by Solomon in Jerusalem. The Temple was the successor to the older Tabernacle, a movable structure which had been built during the period of the wilderness wandering before Israel, under Joshua, entered Canaan. The sacred ark, the most important element in the Tabernacle, had later been located at Shiloh where "the temple of Yahweh" (I Sam. 1:9) was located in the days of Samuel. Shiloh was destroyed during the battles between Israelites and Philistines, and the ark had no permanent abode until David brought it to Jerusalem (II Sam. 6:1-19). From that time to the present, Jerusalem has been considered the religious center of Jewish life and the only appropriate place for the Holy Temple.

No Temple was built in the Jewish settlements of Babylon. The exiles did need to have occasions of fellowship in prayer and Bible study to augment their personal devotional times. Out of this very real need the institution known as the synagogue gradually developed. The synagogue became the community center for Jewish life.

During the Exile there arose a change in the linguistic habits of the Jews. Aramaic, the language of diplomacy in the Persian Empire, became the vernacular of the Jews — both those who returned to Palestine and those who remained in the eastern provinces of the Empire.[3]

Jews who spoke only Aramaic would not be able to understand the Hebrew Scriptures without an interpreter. The custom arose of reading the Hebrew Bible in the synagogue service, after which an explanation would be given in the vernacular Aramaic. This oral explanation in time became a discourse, interpreting and applying the Biblical message. Generations later these explanations, or "targums" were themselves written down, but in their early history they were simple explanations of the Biblical text, ranging from word-by-word translations to quite free paraphrases. More liberties were permitted with the prophetic litera-

---

3. See pp. 53-54.

ture than with the Torah which was accorded the highest degree of inspiration in Jewish thought.

The reading of the Scripture was probably preceded by a prayer. In later Jewish practice the reading from the Torah was preceded by the recitation of the *Shema'* — Deuteronomy 6:4-9; 11:13-21; and Numbers 15:37-41. The *Shema'* gets its name from the Hebrew word "hear," the first word of Deuteronomy 6:4-9 which begins, "Hear, O Israel!"

The institution of the Sabbath, frequently neglected by the pre-exilic communities, became the hall-mark of Judaism during the exilic period. From sundown on Friday to sundown on Saturday the Jew refrained from all work. The Sabbath became a day of rest and worship. In addition to the sacred festivals of the Levitical calendar, the Jews of the exile observed fasts in memory of the national calamities attending the fall of Jerusalem (Zech. 7:3, 5; 8:19). Later the feast of Purim was observed to commemorate the victory of the Jews over their foes in Persian times (Esther 9:27-32).

Corporate worship did not take the place of personal devotion for the godly Jew. Daniel made it a practice to pray three times daily with his face turned toward Jerusalem (Dan. 6:11). Confession of sin and prayers for divine compassion were certainly stimulated by the Exile. Those who, in a spirit of haughtiness, presumed upon God's goodness in pre-exilic times would now see their plight in the light of His holiness. The author of Lamentations cried out, "Turn thou us unto thee, O Lord, and we shall be turned; renew our days as of old" (Lam. 5:21).

It would be dangerous to generalize on the attitude of Babylonian Jews toward their idolatrous associates. Some, probably, had little contact with their non-Jewish neighbors. We do know, however, of many Jews who rose to important positions in the political and business world of the time. Daniel in the courts of Babylon and Persia; Nehemiah the cupbearer to Artaxerxes Longimanus; and Esther the queen serve as notable examples of Jews who were in no sense isolated. We also know that some Jews made a name and fortune for themselves in the world of commerce. The business archives of the Murashu family of Nippur provide an early example of Jews who became successful men of business.[4]

---

4. Cf. H. V. Hilprecht and A. T. Clay, *Business Documents of Murashu Sons of Nippur Dated in the Reign of Artaxerxes I* and Albert T. Clay, *Business Documents of Murashu Sons of Nippur Dated in the Reign of Darius II.*

One result of this new chapter in Jewish life was the impact which Jews had on their non-Jewish associates. Prior to the Exile conversion was largely a matter of living in the land of Israel and assimilating Israelite culture. Ruth the Moabitess determined to serve Naomi's God when she returned with her to Bethlehem, whereas Orpah, Ruth's sister-in-law, returned to Moab and served the gods of Moab (Ruth 1:14-16). During and after the Exile, however, Judaism became a missionary religion. The Jews looked with scorn on the idolatry which once had been so great a temptation to their fathers. They saw idolatry as something evil not only for themselves as Jews, but for all men. A significant and growing number of converts or "God-fearers" looked upon Judaism as the true religion and turned their backs upon paganism. The early church found a ready audience that had been providentially prepared by post-exilic Judaism for the preaching of the Christian gospel.

BIBLIOGRAPHY

PRIMARY SOURCE MATERIAL

Translations of historical texts of Nebuchadnezzar, Nabonidus, and Cyrus by A. Leo Oppenheim in: J. B. Pritchard, ed., *Ancient Near Eastern Texts Relating to the Old Testament* (Princeton, 1955).

Translations of the Babylonian Chronicle by D. J. Wiseman; the Jehoiachin Tablets by W. J. Martin, and historical texts of Nebuchadnezzar, Nabonidus and Cyrus by T. Fish in: D. Winston Thomas, ed., *Documents from Old Testament Times* (London: Thomas Nelson, 1958).

Translations of the Babylonian Chronicle:
D. J. Wiseman, *Chronicles of Chaldaean Kings:* (626-566 B.C.) in the *British Museum* (London: Trustees of the British Museum, 1956).

Translations of the Lachish Letters:
Harry Torczyner, *Lachish I: The Lachish Letters* (London: Published for the Trustees of the Late Sir Henry Wellcome by the Oxford University Press, 1938).
D. Winston Thomas, "Letters from Lachish," in: D. Winston Thomas, ed. *Documents from Old Testament Times* (London: Thomas Nelson, 1958).
W. F. Albright, "The Lachish Ostraca," in: J. B. Pritchard, ed., *Ancient Near Eastern Texts Relating to the Old Testament* (Princeton, 1955).

The histories of Herodotus of Halicarnassus have been edited by A. D. Godley. They appear as Loeb Classical Library volumes 117, 118, 119, and 120. A popular translation by Aubrey de Selincourt appears as L34 in the Penguin Classics Series.

Translations of Business Documents:
> H. V. Hilprecht and A. T. Clay, *Business Documents of Murashu Sons of Nippur Dated in the Reign of Artaxerxes I (464-424 B.C.)* (Philadelphia: Babylonian Expedition of the University of Pennsylvania, 1898).
>
> Albert T. Clay, *Business Documents of Murashu Sons of Nippur Dated in the Reign of Darius II (424-404 B.C.)* (Philadelphia: Babylonian Expedition of the University of Pennsylvania, 1904).

SPECIAL STUDIES

The Babylonian Chronicle:
> David Noel Freedman, "The Babylonian Chronicle," *The Biblical Archaeologist*, XIX, 3 (Sept., 1956), pp. 50-60. Also in *The Biblical Archaeologist Reader*, edited by G. Ernest Wright and David Noel Freedman (New York: Doubleday Anchor Books, 1961).

The Lachish Letters:
> W. F. Albright, "The Oldest Hebrew Letters: the Lachish Ostraca," *Bulletin of the American Schools of Oriental Research*, No. 70 (1938), pp. 11-17.
>
> ———, "A Re-examination of the Lachish Letters," *ibid.*, No. 73 (1939), pp. 16-21.
>
> ———, "The Lachish Letters after Five Years," *ibid.*, No. 82 (1941), pp. 18-24.

Slavery:
> Isaac Mendelsohn, *Legal Aspects of Slavery in Babylonia, Assyria and Palestine. A Comparative Study, (3000-500 B.C.)* (Williamsport, Pa.: The Bayard Press, 1932).

Babylonian Religion:
> Jean Bottero, *La Religion Babylonienne* (Paris: Presses Universitaires de France, 1952).
>
> Edouard Dhorme, *Les Religions de Babylonie et d'Assyrie* (Paris: Presses Universitaires de France, 1949).

Ancient Science:
> O. Neugebauer, *The Exact Sciences in Antiquity* (Providence: Brown University Press, 1957). Also published in the Harper Torchbook Series (New York: Harper & Brothers, 1962).

Samaritans:
> J. A. Montgomery, *The Samaritans: The Earliest Jewish Sect* (Philadelphia: The John C. Winston Co., 1907).
> Moses Gaster, *The Samaritans* (London: Oxford University Press, 1925).

Chronology:
> Richard A. Parker and Waldo H. Dubberstein, *Babylonian Chronology, 626 B.C. — A.D. 75* (Providence: Brown University Press, 1956).

Nabonidus and Belshazzar:
> Raymond Philip Dougherty, *Nabonidus and Belshazzar: A Study of the Closing Events of the Neo-Babylonian Empire* (New Haven: Yale University Press, 1929).

Nebuchadnezzar:
> G. R. Tabouis, *Nebuchadnezzar* (London: George Routledge and Sons, 1931).

Darius the Mede:
> H. H. Rowley, *Darius the Mede and the Four World Empires in the Book of Daniel* (Cardiff: University of Wales Press, 1959).
> John C. Whitcomb, *Darius the Mede* (Grand Rapids: William B. Eerdmans Publishing Company, 1959).

SUGGESTIONS FOR FURTHER READING

Archaeology

Albright, W. F., *The Archaeology of Palestine* (Penguin, 1960).
———, *From the Stone Age to Christianity* (Johns Hopkins, 1946).

Barton, G. A., *Archaeology and the Bible* (American Sunday School Union, 1937).

Burrows, M., *What Mean These Stones?* (Yale, 1941).

Chiera, E., *They Wrote on Clay* (University of Chicago, 1938).

Finegan, J., *Light from the Ancient Past* (Princeton University Press, 1959).

Gordon, C. H., *Adventures in the Nearest East* (Phoenix, 1957).

Kenyon, Kathleen, *Archaeology in the Holy Land* (Ernest Benn, 1960).

McCown, C. C., *The Ladder of Progress in Palestine* (Harper, 1943).
———, *Man, Morals and History* (Harper, 1958).

Pritchard, James B., *Archaeology and the Old Testament* (Princeton, 1958).

Thompson, J. A., *Archaeology and the Old Testament* (Eerdmans, 1960).

Unger, M. F., *Archaeology and the Old Testament* (Zondervan, 1954).

Wright, G. E., *Biblical Archaeology* (Westminster, 1957).

Biblical History

Albright, W. F., "The Biblical Period," *The Jews: Their History, Culture, and Religion.* Louis Finkelstein, ed. (Harper, 1949).

Anderson, B. W., *Understanding the Old Testament* (Prentice-Hall, 1957).

Bright, J., *A History of Israel* (Westminster, 1959).

Gordon, C. H., *The World of the Old Testament* (Doubleday, 1958).

Gottwald, Norman K., *A Light to the Nations* (Harper, 1958).

Heinisch, P., tr., Heidt, W., *History of the Old Testament* (Ecumenical Press, 1952).

Kaufmann, Yehezkel, "The Biblical Age," *Great Ages and Ideas of the Jewish People,* Leo W. Schwarz, ed. (Random House, 1956).

Lods, A., *Israel* (Kegan, Paul, Trubner and Co., 1932).

Noth, Martin, *The History of Israel* (Harper, 1958).

Olmstead, A. T., *History of Palestine and Syria to the Macedonian Conquest* (Scribner's, 1931).

Orlinsky, Harry M., *Ancient Israel* (Cornell University Press, 1954).

Oesterley, W. O. E., and Robinson, Theodore, *A History of Israel* (Oxford, 1932).

Pedersen, J., *Israel* (Branner, 1940).

Whitley, Charles Francis, *The Exilic Age* (Westminster, 1957).

ANCIENT NEAR EASTERN HISTORY

Bury, J. B., Cook, S. A., and Adcock, F. E. *The Cambridge Ancient History, III, IV.* (Cambridge, 1953, 1954).

Hall, H. R. H., *The Ancient History of the Near East* (Methuen, 1950).

Moscati, S., *Ancient Semitic Civilizations* (Elek Books, 1957).
————, *The Face of the Ancient Orient* (Routledge and Kegan Paul, 1960).

Babylon and Babylonia

Budge, E. A. Wallis, *Babylonian Life and History* (Religious Tract Society, 1925).

Contenau, Georges, *Everyday Life in Babylon and Assyria* (Edward Arnold, 1954).

Jastrow, Morris, *History of the Civilization of Babylon and Assyria* (J. B. Lippincott, 1915).

Koldewey, Robert, *Das Wieder Erstehende Babylon* (J. C. Hinrichs'sche Buchhandlung, 1925).

Mallowan, M. E. L., *Twenty-five Years of Mesopotamian Discovery* (British School of Archaeology in Iraq, 1956).

Parrot, Andre, *Babylon and the Old Testament* (S. C. M. Press, 1958).
———, *The Tower of Babel* (S. C. M. Press, 1955).

Rogers, Robert William, *History of Babylonia and Assyria* (Eaton and Maines, 1901).

Rutten, Marguerite, *Babylone* (Presses Universitaires de France, 1948).

Under, Eckhard, *Babylon, Die Heilige Stadt* (Walter DeGruyter and Co., 1931).

Egypt

Aldred, Cyril, *The Egyptians* (Thames and Hudson, 1961).

Breasted, James Henry, *A History of Egypt* (Charles Scribner's Sons, 1909).

Gardiner, Alan, *Egypt of the Pharaohs* (Oxford University Press, 1961).

Biography

Cheyne, T. K., *Jeremiah: His Life and Times* (Anson D. F. Randolph, 1888).

Deane, H., *Daniel: His Life and Times* (Anson D. F. Randolph, 1888).

Ellison, H. L., *Ezekiel: The Man and His Message* (The Paternoster Press, 1956).

Rawlinson, George, *Ezra and Nehemiah: Their Lives and Times* (Anson D. F. Randolph, 1890).

INDEX